Italian Fascism

Alexander De Grand

Italian
Fascism

Its Origins
& Development

Third Edition

University of Nebraska Press
Lincoln & London

Library of Congress Cataloging-in-Publication Data
DeGrand, Alexander.
Italian fascism: its origins and development / Alexander DeGrand.—
3rd ed.
p.   cm.
Includes bibliographical references and index.
ISBN 0-8032-6622-7 (pbk.: alk. paper)
1. Fascism—Italy—History.   2. Italy—Politics and government—
1870–1914.   3. Italy—Politics and government—1914–1945.
I. Title.
DG571.D37   2000
320.53'3'0945—dc21
99-047948

To Linda and Alex

Preface to the Third Edition

Curiously, the further historians get from the direct experience of fascism, the more seriously they take its pronouncements and aspirations. Since the first edition of this book in 1982 much work has been done on Fascist culture and the efforts of Mussolini's regime to reshape Italians through the formation of civic religion, manipulation of symbols, mass rallies, and the intrusion of the state into the private sphere. Yet, in some important ways, this book remains anchored in an earlier tradition that stressed economic and social realities. What fascism did has always seemed to me more important than what it said it wanted to do. I remain quite skeptical about claims that fascism seriously remade Italians. The great economic, social, and ultimately political shift came later with the Italian economic miracle of the late 1950s and 1960s. That said, there is no doubt that fascism was one of the twentieth century's three great approaches to the challenge of organizing the new mass society that emerged at the end of the previous century and exploded on the political scene after World War I. Liberal democracy, an extension of nineteenth-century liberalism, continued to stress individual values and interests, which would be represented on the basis of geographical units (electoral districts and colleges), and a plurality of parties and interest groups. By the early 1920s many doubted that such a system would be adequate to keep political society from fragmenting under the impact of the social and economic disruption produced by the Great War. Already in 1917 the Bolshevik revolution suggested an

x *Preface to the Third Edition*

alternative vision of solidarity and unity: the organization of mass society on the basis of one's status as worker or peasant. The class-based Bolshevik ideal not only negated liberal individualism but also other forms of solidarity, such as the nation or race. However, national and racial solidarity formed the core of a third alternative way of organizing mass society. Unity would be imposed, but it would be on the basis of extreme nationalism (fascism) or racism (nazism). A national or racial myth would be the binding ideological glue that would hold society together. As Roger Griffin and others have pointed out, a myth of national or racial rebirth would offer to society a chance to rise out of the crisis, decline, and social fragmentation that menaced Europe after World War I by beginning anew (*The Nature of Fascism* [London: Routledge, 1994], chapter 2).

Europeans during the period from the end of World War I to the outbreak of World War II were preoccupied, even haunted, by a quest for unity and fear of disintegration. The idea that things were coming apart, that some basic mechanism in western civilization had broken down, and that only revolutionary change or heroic measures could set things right again dominated politics on both left and right. Fear that "the center would not hold" led many to search for all-embracing *total* solutions. To this extent fascism proposed, at least in theory, a *totalitarian* vision of the future.

In chapter 10 and the conclusion of this third edition of *Italian Fascism* I will attempt to come to terms with recent approaches to understanding fascism. But this book remains faithful to its original premise that behind the facade of *totalitarismo* the Italian fascist regime remained politically, economically, culturally, and ideologically fragmented in a series of competing fiefdoms and interest groups. Only by looking at the maneuvers and compromises behind the distribution of power within the Fascist system can one understand the failure to impose a truly unitary vision, the persistence of competing versions of fascism, and the ultimate breakdown of the regime.

A book of this sort would never have been written without the research of several generations of scholars who have shaped my views. Most particularly, I would like to thank once again all those who have assisted me in the development of this book and to add to the list William Harris of North Carolina State University, who jumps from Abraham Lincoln to Mussolini just to see how the other half lives; Spencer Di Scala of the University of Massachusetts in Boston; Alice Kelikian of Brandeis University; Richard Drake of the University of Montana; and K. Steven Vincent of North Carolina State University. I would also like to remember my friend Claudio Segrè, whose contribution to the first edition was essential and whose untimely death cut off a wonderful career, and the late Dr. John Baylor, a cancer specialist whose intervention many years ago certainly made the third edition possible. Finally, although I disagreed with many of his interpretations of the Fascist regime and of Mussolini, I owe an enormous debt to Renzo De Felice, without whose work books like this could not have been written.

Preface

On October 29, 1922, when Benito Mussolini completed his violent, semilegal seizure of power in Italy, the Fascist era began in triumph in front of crowds of blackshirts rushed to the capital to cheer their leader. It ended some twenty-two years later on April 29, 1945, in Piazzale Loreto in Milan, where the bodies of Mussolini and his mistress were hung before quite different crowds, mute evidence that the Fascist experience was indeed over. Between those two fateful moments, Mussolini, the ex-socialist who orchestrated the destruction of the Italian socialist movement, the ex-republican who became an honorary "cousin" of the king, the former antimilitarist who led his country into three useless wars, dominated the spotlight of Europe. Both the man and the regime he led were a mass of contradictions. Fascism defied the efforts of contemporaries to define it, just as, today, it remains at the center of historical debate. Perhaps the soundest advice was given in 1938 by Angelo Tasca, who wrote in his *Rise of Italian Fascism* that the best way to define fascism was to write its history. But even the ordering of events demands a point of view. The problem of orientation, if not definition, remains inescapable. Italian fascism was not just a provincial movement in an obscure country, but a phenomenon that exerted an enormous influence on contemporary Europe. For many it represented a model of efficiency, a possible remedy for a liberal capitalist system and a democratic political system gone awry. In short, fascism seemed a possible "third way" between capitalism and communism.

Leaving aside the excessive praise of its proponents, it can be argued that fascism was a doctrine of bourgeois resurgence whose essence was antiliberalism and antisocialism. The core of its ideology was radical nationalism, but it borrowed freely from syndicalist theory for its doctrine of representation in society by economic or social function, from socialism for many of its propaganda and organizational techniques, and from a number of political thinkers for its theory of the political role of elites and their domination of the masses by manipulation of collective psychology. Radical nationalism was a political theory which developed in Italy in the early twentieth century in response to the rise of socialism. It stressed the organic nation over class as the highest expression of human solidarity; war and imperialism rather than class struggle as a means of selecting those peoples worthy of leadership; and elitism and hierarchy within the nation as an antidote to the leveling aspirations of liberal democracy and socialism. The ideology of national syndicalism was an outgrowth of traditional syndicalist theory that based the struggle for revolutionary change on the worker unions, or syndicates, rather than on the socialist party. The national syndicalists argued that Italy could be organized as a society of producers which transcended any particular class. Mixed syndicates composed of manual workers, technical personnel, and management would be the basis for a new political and economic order dedicated to the achievement of maximum national expansion at home and abroad.

Like all definitions, these leave out almost as much as they include. The great problem is to bridge the gap between what the Fascists said they wanted to do and what they actually did. The difficulty is greater in the case of fascism because it was a vague, composite ideology that evoked different responses at various times from even the Fascists themselves. The following pages are an effort to set fascism in its Italian context as a movement quite distinct from German nazism and current Third World developmental dictatorships. Italy's Fascist regime was essentially a conservative response to a crisis within Italian capitalism and to a breakdown of the liberal parliamentary system that had developed in the nineteenth century. But fascism was more than traditional authoritarianism, which had been and still is content to call out the army to clear the piazza. The Italian Fascists were convinced that simple repression in a highly politicized society would be difficult. They sought to use many of the techniques developed by their Socialist party enemies to regain control over the masses. Thus, the Fascist regime experimented with forms of mass action associated with the left, and with techniques of state intervention in economic and social life developed throughout Europe during World War I and again during the depression of 1929. Needless to say, all of this was carried out by trial and error, rather than by an overall plan. How fascism worked in practice must be considered more important than its ideology. This study will focus on the nature of fascism's constituencies, why they adhered to the movement, what they expected, and how they fared.

The dynamism and contradictions of fascism arose from the different aspirations of the various middle-class groups which espoused it. Within the general framework of fascism, programs were advanced to satisfy the aims of large and small landowners, industrialists, white-collar professionals, small merchants, and businessmen. Each part of the middle class had its own brand of fascism as the movement formed between 1919 and 1922. Many of these fascisms were mere pragmatic positions that sought to defend vested interests, whereas others had more intellectual substance.

It is important to keep in mind the distinction between the Fascist movement and the regime. Initially, fascism as a movement was far broader and more varied than was the disciplined and authoritarian regime. The Fascist movement, which became the National Fascist party (PNF) in 1921, was more than just a reaction to the threat of socialist-inspired revolution, although fascism would have been impossible without the radicalization of Italian politics after World War I and the Bolshevik Revolution. The Fascist movement arose to crush the basis of socialist power that threatened the established order in Italy between 1918 and 1920, but fascism was also designed to offer various middle-class groups a vehicle for long-range political action, something the parties of pre-Fascist Italy were unprepared to do.

Through a series of compromises and adjustments carried out between 1922 and 1929, the Fascist regime distributed power and determined how the aims of each of its component parts would be satisfied. This was done by defining a semiautonomous sphere for each major interest group. In short, a series of fascisms was institutionalized into fiefdoms. I have called this multiplicity *hyphenated fascism* because a modifier (Catholic, monarchist, syndicalist, nationalist) was often added to define more precisely where individuals and groups stood within the regime. This view of fascism as a kind of modern feudalism runs counter to the image of unity and solidarity which the Fascists tried to convey. But, however complicated the distribution of power within the regime, fascism was clearly dominated by conservative social and economic forces. Its concrete actions respected the status quo. Fascism in Italy was a rightist approach to the problem of controlled change in an era of mass politics.

The following chapters will establish a theoretical framework for the analysis of Italian fascism (Chapter One), trace the seizure of power (Chapter Two), the consolidation of the dictatorship (Chapter Three), the creation of the system of "fiefdoms" (Chapter Four), the impact of the depression on the Fascist regime (Chapter Five), Fascist foreign policy (Chapter Six), the economic and social development of late fascism (Chapter Seven), the Italo-German alliance and World War II (Chapter Eight), and the Italian Social Republic (Chapter Nine). Ideology and political culture will receive separate treatment in a concluding chapter. The antifascist Resistance, which is so important for Italian history after 1943, will appear only occasionally, as it affected the functioning and choices of the regime. I have kept footnotes to a minimum, but references to further readings and to theories of fascism can be found in the bibliographical essay at the conclusion of the text.

I wish to thank colleagues and friends who offered their time, counsel, and criticism: Marion S. Miller of the University of Illinois, Chicago Circle; Philip V. Cannistraro of Florida State University; Claudio Segrè of the University of Texas; Anthony Cardoza of Loyola University (Chicago); David Miller and Anne Freedman of Roosevelt University; Umberto Giovine and Dana Willetts of Milan, Italy; Eileen Kennedy; and Linda De Grand. I would also like to thank Dr. John Baylor, whose timely intervention made completion of this work possible.

Part One
The Historical Background 1870–1922

Chapter One
The Origins
of Fascism
1870–1918

Italian Fascism was like a large tree whose roots found nourishment and were entwined deep in the soil of modern Italy. To find these roots it is necessary to examine the economic and social structure of Italy after 1870 to understand which elements under certain circumstances favored the fascist movement and brought it to power.

One of the central problems of Italian political development after 1870 has been the relationship between the political, social, and economic elite groups, who created the unified state, and the mass of society, which was poor, illiterate, and excluded from meaningful participation in national politics. This violent contrast between the elite and the mass provided much of the drama of Italian history and has figured as a central theme in Italian political and social thought.

Italian politics can be described in terms of four groups: the political class, dominant interest groups, the intermediate elite, and the mass base. The political class (*classe politica*) refers to those members of parliament and of government who manage public affairs on the highest level. Dominant interest groups (*class dirigente*) are the leading representatives of organized social and economic forces—landowner and industrial associations, the military, the Catholic Church. The intermediate elite is composed of those who link the political class and the dominant interest groups with the rest of society: estate managers, industrial managers, teachers, civil servants, union officials, journalists. Socially, their members are part of the middle and lower bourgeoisie. Finally, the mass base has an urban sector of white- and blue-collar workers, artisans, small businessmen, unskilled marginal workers, and the unemployed, and a rural sector of small farmers, renters, sharecroppers, landless peasants, and migrant workers. As the following chapters will show, a crisis in the relationship between and within each of these levels of Italian society led to the Fascist regime.

The Italian Political Class from Unification to 1900

United Italy resulted from the victory of French and Piedmontese forces over Austria in 1859. In 1860 the Republican Giuseppe Garibaldi conquered the southern Kingdom of the Two Sicilies but ceded these territories to the Piedmontese House of Savoy, which became the ruling dynasty of united Italy. The process of territorial consolidation was completed with the addition of Venice, taken from Austria in 1866, and of Rome, which passed from papal control in 1870. The new state, which emerged after centuries of division into city-states and minor kingdoms, was organized on two contrasting but complementary principles, each compensating for the defects of the other and both working to provide a political system that functioned reasonably well until the outbreak of World War I. The first principle was centralized administration on the model of France. Italy, governed from Rome through an appointed bureaucracy, offered few concessions to regional autonomy. The second was a parliamentary system, built on the provincial and communal loyalties that had controlled political life from the Middle Ages to 1860. In the Italian parliamentary system the government, headed by the prime minister, rested on a parliamentary majority composed of a number of parties and groups that before World War I often had a regional, rather than an ideological, base.

The political class of united Italy reflected the dominant economic and social position of agriculture. It was a much narrower elite, however, than might have been the case if most practicing Catholics had not withdrawn from political life to protest the Italian seizure of Rome from the pope in 1870. Political control by the landed elite was protected by voting arrangements that kept the vast majority of Italians from exercising the franchise. Italian parliamentary liberalism became an ideal way to broker between regional interests. *Trasformismo*, as the system of shifting personal and political alliances was called, was well suited to a political class divided more by local interest than by ideology.

The major challenge facing the Italian political class was that of transforming Italy into a modern society able to compete with the other great powers of late-nineteenth-century Europe. Such a transformation inevitably placed new burdens on the political leadership, which was forced to accommodate the demands of rising social forces for a voice in public affairs. An electoral reform in 1881 admitted large numbers of shopkeepers and some skilled workers to the voting rolls, but many of the new voters were influenced by the radical republican movement, once led by the prophet of democratic nationalism, Giuseppe Mazzini. The decades after 1881 saw the growth of Radical and Republican party contingents in parliament, as well as the development of a socialist movement. Control by the traditional political class appeared to be seriously threatened for the first time, during the 1890s, by political scandal, economic depression, and labor unrest. When the Italian Socialist party (PSI) was formed in 1892, the political elite, under the leadership of prime ministers Francesco Crispi, Antonio Di Rudinì, and Luigi Pelloux, reacted to unrest and nascent proletarian opposition by banning the Socialist party and using the police and army to suppress agitation by workers and peasants. This purely repressive solution, applied between 1893 and 1899, divided the political class and worried modern-minded industrialists, because it seemed at odds with developments elsewhere in Europe, where the extension of political rights was linked with economic progress. Thus, when repression failed in 1900 because of the determined opposition of a coalition of middle-class liberals and radicals and reformist socialists, there was a general consensus that a new effort had to be made to broaden the base of the political system.

Italian Dominant Interest Groups and Economic Development, 1870–1914

Before 1900 Italy remained a largely agrarian society. The legacy of the wars of national unification between 1859 and 1870 was a staggeringly large national debt and a budget deficit that threatened to drive the new state into bankruptcy. Available public funds were used to build the infrastructure of roads and rails that were required for further growth. Although part of this investment capital came from foreign banks, a great percentage had to come from the agrarian sector in the form of heavy taxes that fell hardest on an already impoverished peasantry. The initial process of state building increased the alienation of workers and peasants from a state which offered them no voice and few tangible benefits. In fact, during the years immediately following unification, whole provinces of southern Italy were put under martial law to repress a wave of social banditry that cost as many lives as the earlier campaigns against Austria.

The process of state construction also strained regional loyalties. The North tended to benefit most from public and private investment. Favored by ties to European markets and control over the state machinery, northern industry and agriculture increased their lead over the more backward South. In short, Italian economic growth was marked by great inequities between classes and regions.

But, even in the North, industrialization was slow. Protective tariffs were introduced in 1878 and gradually increased after 1887. Despite this protection, industry had to struggle to overcome a late start and lack of raw materials. In fact, while the gap between the North and the South increased between 1860 and 1900, so too did the distance between advanced industrial Europe and Italy. Only with the remarkable surge forward after 1898 did Italy achieve a long period of sustained economic growth. Between 1896 and 1908, the growth rate ranged from 5 to 8 percent annually. Agriculture made great progress in the rich Po Valley, where the introduction of new techniques and a reorganization of the agricultural labor force significantly increased grain production. Industry achieved even more impressive results, as emphasis shifted from textiles to three new growth areas: steel and related mechanical industries, chemicals, and electricity.

Italy's expansion resembled that of other late-nineteenth-century developing countries. There was a high degree of concentration and cartelization, a close connection between great banks and the new industrial sectors, and a parallel link between the banks, industry, and the state. By the 1890s, new banking institutions, like the Banca Commerciale (1894) and the Credito Italiano (1895), geared to industrial financing on the German model, were introduced into Italy. The leadership of these highly concentrated banking and industrial combines urgently pressured the state for tariff protection, purchases, and other subsidies.

Thus, between 1860 and 1914 Italy entered a transitional period in which major shifts in economic, religious (the alienation of Catholics from the new state), and social power were taking place. Tension existed between regions and between representatives of more established interests and new groups of industrial and agrarian entrepreneurs. Such shifts inevitably produced stress between the dominant interests and the political class, which was reflected in the succession of crises during the 1890s.

Italy also tended to follow the pattern of other industrial nations in which the dominant interest groups organized into ever more specific economic associations to act as pressure groups on the political structure. At no time, however, before World War I did dissatisfaction with the activities of the political class reach the point that the leaders of industry and agriculture felt the need to intervene directly in the political process. Only after 1918, faced with the threat of revolution, did Italy's economic elite reluctantly seek new political leaders who could restore a workable relationship between the political class and the dominant interest groups.

Intermediate Elites in Prefascist Italy

The intermediate elite groups—all those who have a managerial function in society, transmit orders or ideas, enforce discipline or organize services—are of vital importance for the study of Italian fascism. The Italian Marxist Antonio Gramsci called them "organic intellectuals." He believed that essential social and economic forces create around themselves intermediate categories that explain or justify the needs of the dominant interests to the rest of society. These organic intellectuals are necessary for the smooth operation of society. They provide the middle-level personnel for the political parties, labor unions, and business. They are the journalists, teachers, and professionals who transmit ideologies. At the lowest level they are the estate managers and shop foremen who keep production going by enforcing work discipline. In short, the intermediate elite serves as the link between the mass base and both the dominant interests and the political class.

The steady growth of the lower-middle class, the seedbed of the intermediate elite of both left and right, has been a major social tendency of twentieth-century Italy. Between 1901 and 1921 gains were made in the numbers of white-collar workers in state and private bureaucracies, teachers, small businessmen, and merchants. Even peasant proprietors, who had declined somewhat in numbers at the beginning of the century, increased rapidly during and just after World War I.

This growth was not without problems, however. Italy was producing large numbers of highly educated people for a society with a relatively low level of economic development and a high rate of illiteracy. From the 1880s onward there existed a chronic surplus of high school and university graduates. Traditionally, the Italian middle class had protected itself by using its monopoly over education as a route to upward mobility. Reliance on education in the context of a relatively traditional economy led to an excess of professionals, from lawyers to engineers and architects. Competition for any white-collar position was fierce, and the government was the employer of last resort. Faced with increasingly difficult conditions in the labor market, the Italian middle class viewed control of the political system as essential to maintaining its competitive position. The growing demands of the elite of organized workers for political power represented a direct threat to middle-class status.

From 1900 to 1922 large numbers of middle-class intermediate elite groups responded to the pressures of unemployment and potential proletarianization by using ideology as a weapon. Youth movements, like those of nationalism and fascism, were perfect examples of protest directed at the current political leadership that was held responsible for the crisis. Whatever the importance they gave to social and economic programs, Italian youth protest movements proposed alternative methods of selecting a political class and of linking it with the mass base. But, as the Italian sociologist Paolo Sylos Labini has pointed out, intermediate elites are normally extremely conscious of their economic or social function. They envisage solidarity along vertical or hierarchical lines (loyalty to professions, institutions, or careers rather than to class) which in the case of fascism led them to seek out corporative solutions to political problems.

Similar tensions existed in rural Italy as well. Rapid economic growth created a fundamental disruption of peasant society. A new class of rural entrepreneurs and estate stewards developed who were determined to maintain control of the work force as they introduced new agricultural and marketing techniques. Opposed to these plans were a growing number of landless day laborers in the key areas of advanced agriculture, such as the Po Valley. Although most of central and southern Italy changed more slowly before the war than did the North, events in the Po region indicated that this would be only a temporary respite. Efforts by the Catholic peasant leagues to organize sharecroppers and for the Socialist peasant unions to organize the growing numbers of poor day laborers and tenant farmers introduced an explosive element into the countryside. New intermediate elite groups of peasant organizers were emerging in rural areas as part of a network of labor unions and cooperatives. The failure of the liberal state to integrate a large part of the northern agricultural population into the existing social and political institutions led to the creation of organizations outside of and hostile to the state and to the emergence of new leaders for the excluded sectors of the mass base. The continued growth of peasant unions and cooperatives was a barometer of the revolutionary potential of Italian society. Signs of confrontation between militant peasant and landowner associations were evident before 1914, and the situation erupted into open warfare between 1918 and 1920.

The Mass Base

Within the broad urban and rural categories of the mass base are several social classes and occupational, geographic, and religious subdivisions. Each individual belongs to several of these categories (unions, professional organizations, churches, neighborhood groups, recreational organizations) and is linked to the dominant interests by means of a direct relationship with the intermediate elites (union officials, managers, clergy). During periods of upheaval, such as massive and rapid industrialization and urbanization, war, or serious depression, the masses may be cut off from traditional relationships and thrust into new ones. Delayed modernization in Italy slowed this process of uprooting, but the movement picked up steam during the boom years before World War I and offered a possibility of revolution after 1918. The Italian situation was all the more precarious because the Catholic Church, which could have played a role in integrating the peasantry into the established order, itself had an ambiguous, often hostile, relationship with Italian political institutions. But it was the organization by the Socialists of peasants and industrial workers that radically threatened the links between the mass base of Italians and the existing political and economic order.

The expanding industrial system attracted large numbers of peasants to the cities. Between 1881 and 1911, the population of towns of more than 20,000 inhabitants increased from 23.7 percent to 31 percent. The male population in manufacturing grew by 400,000 between 1900 and 1911, although there was a percentage decline in the number of female workers because of the relative slippage of the textile industry, a major employer of female labor. Despite the rapid growth, Italy was far from becoming a modern industrial economy. Most workers in manufacturing were artisans in small factory units or homes. It has been estimated that of the 27 percent of the population engaged in industry in 1911, workers in the building trades, and in textile, wood, straw, and food-processing industries outnumbered metal, mechanical, and chemical workers by two to one. Increases in the modern factory population were limited largely to the northern industrial triangle of Turin, Milan, and Genoa, while most of the peninsula remained a bastion of cottage and craft industry. Thus, until shaken by economic crisis and labor agitation after the war, most industrial and agrarian leaders did not actively seek an alternative to the existing political system.

The muted consciousness of a clear revolutionary threat before World War I was due in part to the objective difficulties faced by the Italian Socialist party, which after its formation in 1892 was plagued by organizational deficiencies and by the poverty and divisions of the working class. Despite an increase in parliamentary representation between 1900 and 1913, from sixteen to fifty-two seats, the party's membership remained small, and concentrated in the advanced North. Trade unions represented only a tiny fraction of the industrial work force, estimated by the 1911 industrial census at 2.3 million (a million and a half of whom worked in production units of no more than ten people). If there were a few fairly strong, modern unions, such as the Metal Workers' Federation (FIOM), formed in 1901, most of the unions were poor and badly organized. The creation of the General Confederation of Labor (CGL) in 1906 marked a great step forward, but progress remained difficult, and by 1911 its member unions enrolled just under 400,000 workers.

The growth of unions and the steady increase of strike activity among industrial workers were paralleled by similar developments in rural Italy. Class conflict was extraordinarily intense in areas of modern agriculture, like the Po Valley, where peasant unions were vying with landowners for control of the labor force. It was the extent of peasant unrest which was the most ominous sign of decay in the pre-World War I Italian state.

The Giolittian Alternative: The Limits of Liberal Reform

Between 1900 and 1913, an effort to relieve some of the tensions and to enlarge the base of the Italian political system was undertaken by Giovani Giolitti, Italy's greatest liberal prime minister. Giolitti, who rose to power through the state bureaucracy, was an extremely practical administrator and a master of parliamentary maneuver. He so shunned rhetorical flourishes in a country which thrived on them that a passing reference to Dante was enough to cause consternation in parliament. Giolitti's strategy was to shore up Italy's representative institutions by forming new and effective links between the political class and industrial and agricultural interests. To accomplish this aim he used a combination of timeworn and innovative methods. The most traditional means was Giolitti's manipulation of state patronage and favors, in alliance with local landlords, to produce electral majorities in rural southern constituencies. Giolitti also forged a bloc of elite state administrators, bankers, and modern-minded northern industrialists by his program of tariff protection, increased national defense expenditures, labor peace, and mild economic nationalism.

To remedy the alienation at the base of society Giolitti sought to repair the relationship between the political class and the Catholic Church. In this way, he hoped to win the support of the rural clergy to reinforce his hold over a rapidly changing electorate. Finally, Giolitti tried to co-opt the General Confederation of Labor and the reformist-led Italian Socialist party into his system by offering state neutrality in private labor disputes and aid to worker cooperatives and self-help ventures that had nonrevolutionary aims and leadership. Had this political maneuver succeeded, it might have assured the liberal state the support of the new intermediate elite which had developed within the Socialist labor and party structures.

The Giolittian era from 1901 to 1914 was a product of unprecedented prosperity and economic growth. But the fragility of Giolitti's system became apparent under the impact of three successive blows: a depression in 1907–1908 and slower growth thereafter; the decision to go to war with the Ottoman Empire over Libya in 1911; and the introduction of universal manhood suffrage in 1912. These pressures snapped Giolitti's political chain at its weakest link. In 1912, at the Socialist party congress of Reggio Emilia, the revolutionary left took advantage of the strong antimilitarist and antiimperialist feelings within the working class that had been stirred by the Libyan war. The whole framework of debate within the Socialist party shifted leftward, and the revolutionaries took control. The new leadership was violently hostile to Giolitti and to any cooperation with the bourgeois state.

The introduction of universal manhood suffrage in 1912 upset the balance of liberal politics. The existing liberal or constitutional monarchist associations were not prepared for the vast increase in the electorate, which skyrocketed from just over three million voters to almost nine million. More than ever Giolitti needed the support of the Catholics, which he obtained for the 1913 elections at the cost of alienating the anticlerical left wing of his governmental coalition. A series of bitter labor disputes in 1913 further weakened his hold over the political system. In March 1914 Giolitti resigned, and a new right-center government was formed by Antonio Salandra, a conservative who was determined to create an antisocialist middle-class bloc to govern Italy.

New Bourgeois Militancy: 1900-1911

Frustration with the Giolittian alternative and with the general state of Italian politics was common among young middle-class Italians, who watched as the newly organized blue-collar workers began to narrow the gap between industrial and white-collar salaries. An angry mood developed against a political class that was unable to cope with the new socialist menace. After 1903, discontent took the form of an aggressive nationalism. The nationalists rebelled against Italy's status as the weakest of the great powers and advocated a strong imperialist foreign policy. They attributed Italy's weakness to the parliamentary system, which allowed mere numbers to triumph over ability. The young bourgeois critics indignantly rejected Giolittian reformism in favor of a more aggressive response to socialism. Politics became a test of will between classes, and violence was a natural expression of such a contest. The antidemocratic, elitist, imperialist ideology of extreme bourgeois politics was essentially a call to replace the old political class with new men who could win the struggle for the allegiance of the Italian masses against the socialists and who could lead a united nation on the road to imperial expansion. The ideology was first elaborated in small journals, like Enrico Corradini's *Il Regno* (1903), but gained strength after the depression of 1907. Bourgeois protest moved beyond cultural criticism to challenge the existing political class with the formation of the Italian Nationalist Association in 1910. In the years before 1914, the nationalist movement, under the guidance of Luigi Federzoni, Alfredo Rocco, and Enrico Corradini, sought to express industrial and agrarian disenchantment with Giolitti.

Ferment also spread to bourgeois economic and professional organizations, such as the Federazione Nazionale Insegnanti Scuola Media, the major secondary-school teacher organization, which included among its members several future architects of Fascist educational policy. The most notable of these critics was Giovanni Gentile, the first minister of public instruction under Mussolini, who was convinced as early as 1910 that Italian political leadership had failed because the educational system which produced it was inadequate. Only by completely restructuring the schools and by limiting access to higher education could elite groups be saved from submersion in the masses.

Industry began to organize more efficiently in these years. Faced with the unionization of workers, industrialists followed the pattern of their counterparts in other industrial societies. In 1906 the Turin Industrial League was created and became the prototype for similar organizations that followed in other northern cities. In 1910 the various employer federations in the North merged to form the Italian Confederation of Industry and the Association of Italian Joint Stock Companies. This activity reflected concern with the menace of socialism and the feeling that the political class was not responsive enough to industrial needs. Similar militant landowner organizations had been created around Parma and Bologna in the Po Valley with the aim of meeting more forcefully the challenge from the peasant socialist leagues and of pressing agrarian interests on the political class. By the eve of World War I, after more than ten years of economic growth, Italy was as polarized as ever. Despite his best efforts, Giolitti had not successfully broadened the base of the system. Italy was a country at war with itself.

The Crisis of the Old Order

World War I marked a rupture in the course of Italian political development, not in the sense that the war created anything new, but rather because it accelerated the various social, political, and economic tendencies already in operation. From August 1914 to May 1915, a struggle took place between those Italians who, for a variety of reasons, wanted intervention on the side of England and France and those who advocated neutrality between contending blocs. Two broad coalitions faced each other. In favor of neutrality were the Catholic Church, the Italian Socialist party, and the political allies of Giolitti. Pressing for war on the side of the Entente was a heterogeneous coalition: dissident revolutionary socialists and syndicalists, who argued that war would hasten the coming of the revolution; radical and republican democrats, who admired England and France; and the king, conservative supporters of the Salandra government, and the nationalist right, who were all interested in using the war to expand territorially against Austria and to reinforce the power of the middle class within Italy. This interventionist movement, which foreshadowed later fascism in its combination of right and left, was a revolt of part of the dominant interests and a substantial part of the younger, middle-class intellectuals against the old Giolittian political class and its reformist policies. The interventionists sought to blur political alignments in an attempt to create a new movement, bound by a common nationalist tie. Finally, interventionism appeared to be a victory of determined minorities over the passive masses and the normal political process. But the prowar movement fell short of becoming the vehicle of bourgeois revival. The parties favoring the war were too small to carry out the task of altering the political system and forging new links between the masses and the political class. Like Benito Mussolini, one of the youngest and most dynamic of the interventionists, they were leaders without a following.

The Great Red Hope: Mussolini and Italian Socialism

A remarkable feat of imagination is necessary to recognize the dynamic revolutionary socialist of 1912 in the prematurely old man, wracked by ulcers and feeble of will, who was dragged from a German military convoy by the partisans in April 1945. And nothing in Mussolini's childhood would have indicated the meteoric rise of a poor, lower-middle-class child to political prominence. The future Duce was born in Predappio in the agricultural Romagna region on July 29, 1883. His father was a blacksmith and self-educated revolutionary socialist, and his mother was a teacher, who was determined that her son use education as the means to rise out of obscurity. After completing his studies for a teaching certificate, Mussolini taught elementary school in 1901 before emigrating to Switzerland in 1902, where he worked as a manual laborer and frequented socialist circles. During his two-year stay in Switzerland, Mussolini met several of the leaders of the revolutionary faction of Italian socialism and syndicalism who gave him his first systematic introduction to Marxist thought. Between 1905 and 1909 he served in the army, briefly returned to teaching, and then emigrated once again to the Trentino (the Italian-speaking part of the Austrian Empire), where in 1909 he served as secretary to the local socialist organization.

By 1910 the still almost unknown Mussolini had absorbed a variety of experiences that became the basis for his political outlook as he began his rise within the Socialist party. First, there was the legacy of his socialist and anticlerical father and of his native Romagna, a region marked by violent class conflict and strong anarchist and republican political traditions. Second, Mussolini was shaped by the experience of revolutionary syndicalism. Between 1900 and 1910 he was politically close to syndicalists like A.O. Olivetti and Sergio Panunzio. Although Mussolini never accepted the syndicalists' faith in the revolutionary potential of trade unions, he found extremely appealing their rejection of reformism and advocacy of direct revolutionary action as a means of mobilizing the masses. Third, Mussolini was formed by his readings in the new theories of mass behavior, myths, and crowd psychology, and the function of elite groups in history, which were current in the writings of Vilfredo Pareto, Gaetano Mosca, and Gustave Le Bon. Finally, Mussolini adopted from Italian revolutionary socialism its total rejection of reformism and the stress on the political party rather than the trade union as the means toward revolutionary change. These various influences made Mussolini a somewhat atypical socialist. He was little bound to party orthodoxy or discipline. His violent, restive personality ill concealed a desire to dominate others and an opportunism that worried his revolutionary colleagues. But this same nonconformism made Mussolini an idol of the younger generation of socialists who were dissatisfied with the gradualist tactics of the party leadership before 1912.

More than anything else, Mussolini typified the intellectual disquiet, impatience with procedure, irrationalism, and latent authoritarianism of the bourgeois rebels on the right. His rise within the Socialist party was the perfect meeting of man with moment. Almost unknown in 1909, he used the leadership of the socialist federation of Forlì and the crisis of the reformist leadership of the Socialist party during the Libyan war to break through to the top. Yet his success led directly to his downfall as a socialist leader. Mussolini rose as a brilliant journalist, a man who manipulated the masses but who did not belong to them either in intellectual outlook or in sympathy. Eventually, he misjudged the hold which personal magnetism had created.

Still, in 1912, Mussolini cut a remarkable figure. Intense, impetuous, and unorthodox in both his politics and personal life, he became a rallying point for those young socialists who sought new ideas and approaches. When the revolutionaries took over the leadership of the party after the Congress of Reggio Emilia in 1912, they were forced to offer the editorship of the *Avanti!*, the party newspaper, to Mussolini. It was a decision taken with some misgivings by his party colleagues, both because it was the most visible post in the party and because they distrusted Mussolini. The latter, who, if nothing else, was an extraordinary journalist, promptly opened the pages of the *Avanti!* to new writers and ideas. He cared little for ideological coherence. The marriage between Mussolini and his more orthodox comrades on the revolutionary left could not last. For all their faults, the true leaders of Italian socialism were marked by loyalty to principle and by a deep sympathy for the working class. They instinctively desired to move with the people, not against them or ahead of them.

The crisis of World War I was the turning point in Mussolini's career. The majority of Socialists would not violate their antimilitarist and internationalist convictions, yet they lacked a strategy to turn opposition to the war into a revolutionary movement. As a result, the party's stand became one basically of passive opposition to the war. At first, Mussolini responded to World War I much like the other Socialists, but he soon wavered and adopted a position similar to that of the bourgeois rebels who sought to use the conflict to destroy the Giolittian political system. In a famous editorial in the *Avanti!* on October 18, 1914, called "From Passive to Operative and Active Neutrality," Mussolini tried to prod the Socialists toward a prowar stand. He argued that the party could not remain anchored to principle, nor could the proletariat absent itself from a fundamental national decision. Such arguments failed to shake the profound antimilitarism and humanitarianism of the party, which saw no advantage to the proletariat in joining the useless slaughter. Mussolini, embarking on the greatest gamble of his life, refused to alter his views and was ousted as editor of the *Avanti!* and expelled from the party. A political figure of Mussolini's ability and fame was a valuable commodity for the economic and political forces pressing for Italian intervention in the war on the side of England and France. When Mussolini returned a month later as editor of *Il Popolo d'Italia*, a newspaper financed by industrialists favorable to the war and, for a time, by the French, his former comrades greeted him with a chorus of "Who pays you?" Almost overnight, Mussolini's hold over the workers vanished. The gap between the former editor of the *Avanti!* and his party became a chasm. Mussolini began the passage that would carry him from revolutionary socialism to "national" syndicalism and then to a simple nationalism that had little in common with socialism.

The Crisis of the Great War

Italy entered the war on May 24, 1915, under the terms agreed upon in the Treaty of London of April 26 by the Italian and the Entente governments. The treaty promised Italy a frontier on the Brenner Pass in the Northeast, annexation of Trieste and the Istrian Peninsula (but not Fiume), part of the Dalmatian coast in what is now Yugoslavia, a dominant position in Albania, and unspecified colonial concessions. The decision for war was taken despite substantial neutralist sentiment in the country and in parliament. The prime minister, Salandra, counted on a neat, short, victorious war; instead it was long, messy and destructive beyond all expectations and caused a major upheaval in Italian society. During the three and one-half years of war, from May 1915 to November 1918, Italy mobilized 5.7 million soldiers, the majority of which were peasants. Most went into the infantry, which absorbed 95 percent of the casualties. As the war continued, the bitterness of the peasant soldier toward those who remained behind increased, and a wedge was driven between the peasants in the army and the industrial workers, who often received exemptions for war production. Despite attaining some reforms in tenant contracts and gains in land ownership, peasants felt alienated from other sectors of Italian society. The military also mobilized large numbers of young middle-class students and professionals. Between 1914 and 1918,

160,000 new officers were brought into the army. For the minority of active interventionists within the officer corps, life was extremely difficult. Common soldiers resented the enthusiasm of the advocates of war, and former leftists with revolutionary pasts, like Mussolini, were held in suspicion by the soldiers and government alike.

The war split the political class. Giolitti, who commanded almost a majority in parliament, had been opposed to the war. None of the successive governments—Salandra to June 1916, Paolo Boselli to October 1917, and Vittorio Emanuele Orlando to June 1918—could govern with or against Giolitti. The resulting paralysis of the political class had the effect of increasing the hostility between young and old, between those who rejected parliament and those who had made their careers in it. The links that held liberal Italy together began to break.

Only after the disastrous defeat at the hands of the Austrians at Caporetto in October and November 1917 did the political class respond to the new dimension of the war. A major propaganda effort was directed at the soldiers for the first time. That last year of the war, from October 1917 to November 1918, fundamentally altered Italian politics. First, in order to raise morale after Caporetto, parliament made promises to the peasant soldiers that increased the social cost of the war. Aspirations of the peasantry for land reform, and the hopes of the young bourgeois officers for changes in the political system, seemed within reach. Second, Italian war aims in the Balkans, Asia, and Africa, which alone could justify the suffering, were threatened by the entry of the United States into the war in April 1917 and by the rise of central European and Balkan nationalism. For the extreme Italian nationalists, who measured success in terms of territory, the chief rationale for the war was in jeopardy. Finally, the Bolshevik Revolution sparked a new wave of unrest and provided a model of change that the Socialist party would henceforth try to translate into Italian experience.

Conclusion

By the end of the war the major problem facing the Italian political class and the dominant interests was the restoration of social control over the urban and rural working class. The old electoral and parliamentary mechanism had broken down under the stress of war. As we shall see, the solution to this problem came not in the form of a military coup, but as something entirely new and much more complicated. Instead of suppressing social unrest by calling out the army or police, fascism created a private army alongside the existing state apparatus. This Fascist alternative mobilized large numbers of discontented young officers, students, and professionals in the cities and towns, and estate managers, small farmers, and some sharecroppers in the rural areas. This became the basis of the Fascist paramilitary force that defended the existing social order against the threat of revolution. The leaders of the Fascist party hoped to use this new form of political warfare to take over the state and sweep away the old political class. The Church, industry, and the military accepted these changes for several reasons. Their impatience with the old liberal political class had grown to such an extent that they saw in the new Fascist movement a way of re-asserting control over the workers and peasants. There was also a consensus by 1922 among the same dominant interest groups that political conflict had to be suspended while the institutions and leadership of the political class were reorganized. Thus, after 1922, the multiparty, competitive political system gradually gave way to the monopoly of the Fascist party. In the eyes of the established order, such a single-party regime had a triple task: to rebuild the links between the political class and the mass base, to create new solidarities between the political class and the dominant interests, and to provide a period of calm during which these changes might come about, even if that meant slowing the tempo of Italian economic and social development.

Once in power, the Italian Fascists never moved beyond a relatively loose single-party structure, a "leaky" totalitarianism. The basic technique of Fascist rule was improvisation. Power was fragmented within the formally unified structure of the regime. Such a system satisfied the needs of the dominant interest groups (church, military, industry, agriculture, the monarchy), which had no interest in massive social experimentation. Yet, while the regime satisfied its constituencies, it suffered from the lack of any strong, unifying principle except the personal myth of the Duce. Far from being a revolutionary system of government, Italian fascism succeeded best when it opted for compromise within the conservative order. When later it tried to compete with the truly totalitarian regime of Nazi Germany, all the weaknesses and backwardness inherent in the Italian situation came to the fore.

The regime of fiefdoms, or "hyphenated" fascisms, was in reality a system of collective irresponsibility. The harvest of fascism was retarded political development, the exclusion of a large part of society from any meaningful role in economic or social life, and, ultimately, war and physical ruin. It would be a high price to pay for "a place in the sun."

Chapter Two
The Postwar Crisis and the Development of Fascism
1918–22

The Impact of War

The effect of the Great War on Italy's economy and society was dramatic. Already before the outbreak of the fighting, the tendency toward industrial concentration in the most highly developed sectors of the economy was pronounced. During the war, economic mobilization further strengthened the hold that certain firms had over the metal and engineering sectors (Ilva and Ansaldo) and automobiles (Fiat). Industrial production expanded rapidly between 1915 and 1918, too rapidly, in fact, to be sustained by the postwar domestic market alone. Disrupted international trade, the scarcity of raw materials, and the end of the system of allied cooperation made the outlook for Italian industry extremely gloomy. The balance of trade figures for 1919 revealed that exports covered only 36 percent of imports. The cost of living was four times the level of 1913, while the budget deficit reached unprecedented heights. Ties between industry and the government became ever more important as the economy faced the prospect of demobilization and recession. But the political system was caught between irreconcilable demands. Organized workers were determined to protect their jobs and standard of living against the ravages of unemployment and inflation. At the moment of the armistice, there were more than 3 million men under arms and 500,000 prisoners in Austrian hands. Rapid demobilization drove unemployment to 2 million by the end of 1919. Industrialists were determined to beat back demands for higher wages, as well as the revolutionary aspirations of the workers to participate directly in the management of industry.

Large segments of Italian society no longer responded to traditional means of political control. The full impact of universal manhood suffrage was now felt as parliamentary elections were held for the first time since 1913 under a system of proportional representation that put a premium on party organization. Three movements pressed to take advantage of the new situation. The Italian Socialist party emerged from the war in a stronger state, but was hampered by its inability to coordinate its reformist and revolutionary wings, by a lack of support in southern Italy, and by the failure to mesh its rural and urban organizations. The Catholics launched their own political party, the Italian Popular party (PPI), formed in January 1919 under the leadership of a Sicilian priest, Don Luigi Sturzo. The PPI expressed a new awareness on the part of Church authorities that political organization was vital in an era of mass politics. The party's strength among peasants in Lombardy, the Veneto, and Alto Adige gave it a solid electoral base, but the PPI was plagued by deep divisions between right- and left-wing Catholics. The political balance of the party was held by middle-class democrats, who advocated a series of moderate political and social reforms within the existing capitalist system. The party's success depended in large part on the Vatican's support for a semiautonomous and democratic political movement and on the creation of a majority for moderate reform in the polarized postwar situation. Finally, the last of the new forces to emerge on the political scene was the veterans' movement, primarily the large democratic National Association of Ex-combatants. This movement's leadership was composed of demobilized, reform-minded officers who wanted to create new political relationships outside of the traditional party structures. However, organizations like the Association of Ex-combatants failed to reach their peasant and middle-class constituencies (especially in the South) and were wiped out in the elections of 1919.

The Red Years: In Search of the Italian Lenin

The possibility for revolution in Italy never seemed more real than in 1919. The quantum leap forward made by the Socialist party was probably the most impressive political change to result from the war. Membership in the General Confederation of Labor rose from 250,000 in 1918 to 2 million in 1920. In the elections of November 1919, the Socialist party gained almost 2 million votes and 156 seats to become the largest single political force in Italy. Proletarian militancy and expectations were never higher. In 1919 there were 1,663 industrial strikes involving over a million workers; 208 agricultural strikes brought out another half million. The next years saw a continuation of the same trend: 1,881 strikes in industry and 189 in agriculture, involving over a million industrial workers and one million peasants. Between September and November 1919, peasants in central and southern Italy spontaneously began to seize poorly cultivated and uncultivated land. Throughout the country the violent class warfare, which had simmered just below the surface, exploded into what seemed like civil war.

At the congress of the Italian Socialist party, held in Bologna in November 1919, the leadership groped for a way to channel these mobilized masses toward concrete social change. The reformists, strong in the unions and among the Socialist parliamentary delegation, argued against any application of the Bolshevik model to Italy and in favor of a series of reforms that would be undertaken in cooperation with other democratic parties. On the far left, a group of young revolutionaries from Turin, led by Antonio Gramsci, editor of *Ordine Nuovo*, attempted to construct the revolution outside of parliament on the basis of factory councils and worker control of production. The Neapolitan Amadeo Bordiga, who would become the first leader of the Italian Communist party, argued that the correct application of Bolshevik principles to Italy lay in the Leninist organization of the revolutionary party. The majority of Socialists, however, opted for a position between reformism and Leninism that placed priority on the goal of revolution without confronting the organizational and political problems involved in such a choice. These profound differences over strategy paralyzed the Socialist party and isolated it from other political movements. The Socialists were unable either to take advantage of their parliamentary strength to force political change or to use the strike wave to topple the bourgeois state.

Bourgeois Italy Between Retreat and Resurgence: 1919–20

Despite the impressive socialist tide, the political balance had not shifted as dramatically as it seemed. Some of the gains made by the left were merely a result of the divisions of the traditional middle-class parties into supporters and opponents of Giolitti, neutralists and interventionists, and moderates and nationalists in foreign policy. Instead of uniting for the elections of 1919, the bourgeois parties faced the electorate divided and poorly organized. Only after the shocking electoral results, which saw the liberals lose their majority in parliament, did it become clear that the inability of the Catholics and Socialists to govern singly or together would allow the traditional politicians to reemerge as the brokers between old and new forces.

Of the four prime ministers during the postwar era—Francesco Saverio Nitti, Giolitti, Ivanoe Bonomi, and Luigi Facta—only Nitti offered a departure from past practices, but his democratic program was swallowed up by economic crisis and lingering bitterness over the Versailles Peace Conference, where Italy's claims to Dalmatia and to colonial compensation were left unsettled. One hotly contested issue was the future of the city of Fiume at the northern end of the Adriatic Sea, which was claimed by both Italy and Yugoslavia. In September 1919, Gabriele D'Annunzio, Italy's most famous dramatist and a war hero who lost an eye while engaging in spectacular symbolic gestures (like flying over Vienna to launch propaganda leaflets), capped an erratic political career by leading a band of volunteers, recruited from veterans and students, into the disputed city of Fiume. Perhaps only in the confused and tormented years after World War I could such a gesture have been possible, and, even then, it would never have succeeded but for the refusal of the Italian army to stop him and Nitti's inability over many months to end the occupation by force or negotiation. The whole Fiume affair seriously undermined the credibility of the parliamentary regime. D'Annunzio's virtuoso performance in Fiume, from which he issued endless messages to Europe and the world, attracted widespread support from discontented students and veterans, who had earlier been caught up in the campaign for intervention in World War I and now saw the Fiume enterprise as a first step to a "march on Rome" against the political class. Left and right, syndicalists and nationalists, gathered around D'Annunzio to topple the hated parliamentary state. Although the effort failed, in part because of D'Annunzio's defects as a leader, the lack of support from industry and the army, and overall deficiencies in planning, it was clear that these same groups would continue to search for an adequate vehicle through which they could express their grievances.

If the health of the parliamentary system and the traditional middle-class parties was not robust, the economic position of the bourgeoisie was far from hopeless. To compensate for the crisis in political leadership, there was a burst of organizational activity at the economic level on the part of agrarians and industrialists in 1919 and 1920. In April 1919 the General Confederation of Italian Industry (Confindustria) was formed on a national basis to increase the political and economic leverage of heavy industry. Similar associations followed in agriculture, banking, and commerce. Strains between the economic establishment and the political class had become so serious, and the link between the state and business so vital, that these pressure groups reflected the determination to move beyond traditional political activity to protect their interests. What was still lacking in 1919 was the vehicle through which their aspirations for strong government could be realized.

In general, the middle class felt and expressed its economic and social aspirations in a way that distinguished it from the proletariat and landless peasants and made any alliances difficult. The immediate problem was one of social and professional status and resumption of schooling or careers. The educational system continued to turn out graduates in the professions without providing an outlet for their talents. To make matters worse, the number of university graduates was up 42 percent in 1918–19 over the prewar period. There was a 46 percent increase in graduates from the classical liberal arts high schools (*licei*), a 19 percent increase in students in teacher training institutes, and a 256 percent increase in graduates from technical training schools. (This latter figure reflected the tremendous aspirations to improve individual status on the part of lower-middle-class and ambitious worker elements.) Thousands of new teachers, lawyers, architects, and technicians entered the market, while the number of positions increased only slightly.[1]

Economic pressures politicized many professions. Engineers and architects formed professional associations in 1919 and played a major role in the creation of the Confederation of Intellectual Labor, which attempted without success to bring together various professional organizations in a national right-wing pressure group. This new militancy did not work in favor of the left: a socialist-oriented teacher organization failed to win any substantial following. In fact, the Socialist-led strikes of 1919 and 1920 created resentment among the middle class, which saw the strikes as an inconvenience and a threat to its status. Unemployment, inflation, and the expectations engendered by the war among all social classes created an explosive situation. It remained an open question as to who would succeed in lighting the fuse.

The Return of Giolitti: "Remembrance of Things Past"

Giolitti's return to office in July 1920, at the age of seventy-eight, raised hopes that a master politician might, by some stroke of genius, resolve the crisis within the framework of the traditional political class. His government went far to meet the demands for reform by proposing progressive taxation, an inquiry into excess war profits, publication of stock ownership, and the nationalization of the telephone industry. Giolitti aspired to recreate the prewar coalition of reformist unions, northern industry, and agriculture. But the Socialist party was no longer in reformist hands, and the unions had become more radical. A new Catholic party had entered the scene, and its leader, Luigi Sturzo, distrusted Giolitti's motives and strategy. More important, the revolutionary fervor that had convulsed Italy since 1918 reached a climax. Just as Giolitti sought to forge his new system of alliances, the mood of the Italian middle class shifted from passive terror to a bitter determination

1. Marzio Barbagli, *Disoccupazione e sistema scolastico in Italia* (Bologna: Il Mulino, 1974), pp. 173–75.

to destroy the very foundations of socialist power in the countryside and in the city.

The Crisis of 1920

Symbolically, the moment of extreme tension occurred in Milan and Turin, the centers of the factory council movement, and in Bologna, the capital of rural socialism. In September 1920, the auto workers of the FIOM seized the factories in order to prevent an employer lockout during a contract dispute. Giolitti, drawing on past experience, refused to use force and instead worked out a compromise between the employers and the moderate union leaders. But times had changed. What appeared to business leaders as wisdom in 1912 now seemed to be dangerous capitulation. Many industrialists preferred to seek their own solution to the problem of labor unrest and reassertion of control over the work force.

At the same time, the Po Valley was consumed by a brushfire of peasant agitation. In 1920 almost one million peasants belonged to leagues associated with the Catholic Italian Confederation of Labor, and an almost equal number adhered to the Socialist Federterra, which was linked to the General Confederation of Labor. In whole provinces an alternative power structure of union leaders and directors of cooperatives had developed to challenge the control of the large landowners and the traditional political hierarchies. This local power base had one weakness, which only became apparent when the Fascists launched their violent counterattack. Each provincial socialist organization was a world unto itself and could be attacked singly. The leagues found their main support among the desperately poor, landless day laborers and sharecroppers of the Po Valley where, in the provinces of Bologna, Reggio Emilia, Parma, and Ferrara, Socialist leaders swept to power in the municipal elections of November 1920. Control of local government gave the peasant leagues a voice in the area of public works contracts and patronage, which had formally been at the disposition of the landlords.

The peasant leagues sought a collective contract from the landlords that would make their hiring halls the exclusive source of labor for a given province. After a major strike in the autumn of 1920, the leagues emerged victorious, but a sign that the tide was turning came during the municipal elections of November, when the newly formed bourgeois coalitions kept control of all the large cities with the exception of Milan, Bologna, and Livorno. The elections also confirmed the power of the Socialist party, which won control of 2,162 of the 8,300 towns and cities and twenty-six of sixty-nine provinces. Thus, the voting revealed a country divided into two blocs. What was not entirely clear at the time was that the power of the proletarian bloc had peaked, while that of the bourgeoisie was only beginning to manifest itself.

The Emergence of Fascism: 1919–21

Mussolini's switch from a position of neutrality to one of intervention in World War I separated him forever from the socialist movement. Once war was declared, Mussolini served in the military from November 1915 to August 1917, when he was released because of injuries incurred in a grenade incident. During these war years he moved steadily away from his socialist convictions. In August 1918 the newspaper he edited, the *Popolo d'Italia*, which had initially carried the word *socialist* on the masthead, now proclaimed itself the paper "of the producers and soldiers." Instead of advocating allegiances based on class, Mussolini followed out the logic of "national syndicalism" by calling for a new coalition of producers, both bourgeois and proletarian, against the "parasites" in the political class and in the Socialist party.

By the end of the war, however, Mussolini's career was in shambles. He had gambled that a new movement might be launched out of the interventionist alliance. His rupture with the Socialists and his nationalist positions on foreign policy isolated him from the masses while winning few converts among the middle class, which still viewed him as a subversive republican. Most veterans rallied to D'Annunzio, the hero of the moment, for his exploit in Fiume.

Throughout 1919 Mussolini sought vainly to maneuver against the rising socialist tide. His immediate interest was to keep the *Popolo d'Italia* afloat. Of much more long-term significance was his decision to found a new political movement, the Fascio di Combattimento, in Milan on March 23, 1919. The terms *fascio* and *fascist* had no precise significance in 1919. They had been used by radicals in the late-nineteenth century and by groups of all political hues during World War I. The literal meaning is "bunch," or "group," from the bound sticks which the Roman lictor used as a symbol of office. To add to the confusion, the nominally left-wing "fascists" met in the headquarters of the Association of Commerce, Industry, and Agriculture, located on the Piazza San Sepolcro. The new group attracted minimal attention and barely more than a hundred particpants drawn mainly from three groups: arditi (veterans of special combat units); politically minded futurists, members of a cultural movement under the leadership of Filippo Tommaso Marinetti that aimed at bringing art into step with modern, urban, and industrial life; and some dissident socialists and syndicalists from Mussolini's early days. The Fascist program of 1919, which called for the vote for women and eighteen-year-olds, a new republican constitution, the eight-hour day, and worker participation in management, was but a continuation of the leftist interventionism or "national syndicalism" of the wartime era.

What we know as fascism, however, was not born on March 23, 1919, in Milan. The membership and outlook of the initial fascio had little chance of finding political space in Italy. The true birth of fascism came in countless towns throughout rural Italy between the autumn of 1920 and the spring of 1921. After the electoral debacle of November 1919, when the Fascists in Milan received fewer than 5,000 votes out of 275,000, much of the original membership (mainly syndicalists, socialists, and futurists) drifted off. From a low point in December 1919, when there were only 31 fasci (local sections) with 870 members, the movement made a spectacular recovery as the party of bourgeois resurgence. By the end of 1920 there were already 88 fasci with over 20,000 members, and a year later these numbers had grown to 834 fasci with almost 250,000 members. Two forces coalesced to produce this result: an urban movement, led by Mussolini and a few associates from his early days, and a vast movement of agrarian reaction against the Socialist peasant leagues.

Agrarian Fascism, 1920–21: Redemption by Club and Castor Oil

The birth of agrarian fascism coincided with the victory of the peasant leagues after the strike of October 1920. The first major agrarian Fascist group was that of Bologna, reconstituted in October 1920 under the leadership of Leandro Arpinati. The Bolognese fascio sparked a riot at the inauguration of the Socialist administration of Bologna in November that left several dead and wounded, the new city administration suspended, and the landlords ready to break the infrastructure of Socialist power by the physical and political destruction of the peasant unions. If Bologna provided the spark, Ferrara under Italo Balbo, a young veteran and occasional student in political science, gave fascism its first victory, between March and May 1921. The local Ferrarese fascio, recruited from students and lower-middle-class professionals of the city and sons of small landlords, tenants, and estate managers, received its financial support from the large landlords and allied industries, like sugar refining. From Ferrara the movement spread back to Bologna and then throughout the Marches, Romagna, Emilia, Tuscany, and Umbria.

Agrarian fascism was an overwhelming success. In 1920 there were over 1 million strikers in agriculture; the next year only 80,000. To accomplish this turnabout, the Fascists used a combination of stick and carrot. With military precision whole towns were surrounded by Fascist squads, drawn from one, sometimes several, provinces. The headquarters of the peasant leagues and of the Socialist party were burnt and their leaders seized and given lessons in the new patriotism by means of large doses of castor oil and severe beatings on the kidneys—a message which was often fatal. The Socialist historian Angelo Tasca in his *Rise of Italian Fascism* estimated that, during the first six months of 1921, 119 labor chambers, 107 cooperatives, and 83 peasant league offices were attacked and destroyed, the loss of a generation of struggle for a better life. The carrot came in the form of playing one tenant farmer off against another, or sharecroppers against day laborers, by means of favorable contracts outside the unions. The peasants, deprived of protection and desperately poor, lacked the means to resist.

Between April and May 1921, membership in the Fascist movement jumped from 80,000 to 180,000. By the end of the year a network of Fascist organizations emerged in the provinces of northern and central Italy. Each of the major cities became a kind of barony under one or more important Fascist chiefs, or ras (after Ethiopian tribal leaders): Italo Balbo in Ferrara, Leandro Arpinati and Dino Grandi in Bologna, Roberto Farinacci in Cremona, Dino Perrone Compagni in Florence were but a few of the most important ras.

The initial Fascist groups were urban and expanded from the provincial capital into the surrounding countryside. The original fasci were often made up of students, young professionals, and shopkeepers. These lower-middle-class elements united with the larger estate owners and their managers in a common hated of the Socialists, but their aims were somewhat different. The middle-class Fascists wanted to fill the gap left by the collapsing structures of Socialist and Catholic peasant leagues. They envisaged for themselves the role of intermediaries between the masses and the political class. To this end, many, like Balbo and Grandi, adopted theories of Fascist syndicalism and organized peasants into Fascist labor unions. Such ambitions went far beyond those of the vast majority of landowners, who would have been content merely with the destruction of the peasant leagues. The split was not fundamental, but the program of the provincial lower-middle class to use the Fascist party and the unions to forge new links between the masses and the state would be a source of future friction with the conservative establishment.

Fascism in 1920–21: Brains or Brawn?

The Fascist movement became the long-sought instrument of bourgeois resurgence. A survey of 150,000 of the 220,000 members of the Fascist movement, at the time of the third congress in November 1921, showed that one half were war veterans. The only sizable worker group was composed of farm laborers, who made up 24 percent of the members, and merely indicated the success of the terror campaign in rural Italy. The bulk of Fascist support came from the middle class, especially from the younger generation. White-collar workers, teachers, architects, and lawyers were drawn to the movement. Landowners made up 12 percent of the membership. Absent in the first stage of growth were the representatives of heavy industry. The movement was much more a protest of rural and small-town Italy with the participation of urban professionals of the larger centers. Almost one quarter was below voting age, and 20,000 were students.[2]

Like the young leaders of the emerging Fascist peasant organizations, the urban professionals also sought to restructure the political class by a technocratically-oriented Fascist party. The watchword of the young Fascists was *competenze*, or abilities. These veterans and university graduates wrote into the 1921 program of the party provisions for technical study groups *(gruppi di competenza)* to prepare detailed programs for various sectors of state activity. Although the study groups did not get very far, the basic idea of a party that would take upon itself all activities of society was present in the technocratic vision of some of these ardent planners.

That the aims of the lower-middle-class Fascists went beyond those of the agrarian and industrial backers of the movement is beyond doubt. But the conservative establishment faced a dilemma. At first, it only wanted to destroy the alternative power structure created by the Socialists. Once this was done, however, the conservatives faced the difficulty of ensuring that there would be no return to socialism when the crisis was over. How could control over the masses be maintained if the liberal parliamentary system had already proven so inadequate? Mussolini sought to exploit these doubts in 1921 and 1922 as he maneuvered fascism to power. Tensions within the fascist movement, between provincial, agrarian fascism and Mussolini's political leadership, between fascism's leftist, republican rhetoric and the new rightist reality, and between the lower-middle-class aspirations for a vast reorganization of political structures and the relatively conservative aims of Italy's dominant interest groups, could be controlled as long as socialists remained the common enemy. Once power had been achieved, the contradictions within fascism would have to be resolved.

2. Juan Linz, "Some Notes Toward a Comparative Study of Fascism in Sociological Historical Perspective," in *Fascism: A Reader's Guide*, ed. Walter Lacqueur (Berkeley: University of California Press, 1976): 67–69.

The Collapse of the Liberal State: The Elections of 1921

Giolitti's strategy for controlling both socialism and fascism in the interest of the traditional order proved a failure. He sought to manipulate the Fascist movement by splitting its political wing with promises of office, while at the same time permitting its squads to pound the Socialists into a cooperative mood. This design failed when, in the national elections of May 1921, the combined Socialist and Communist vote (the Italian Communist party was formed in January 1921) dropped only slightly from the high point of 1919. The traditional liberal political class emerged from the elections without proving that it could control a mass electorate. Only the Fascists, whom Giolitti had included in his national bloc, did well by winning 36 of the bloc's 120 seats and running ahead of their liberal allies almost everywhere. The elections were followed in November by the third congress of the Fascist movement. The Fascists ratified their new rightist policies and resolved the first conflict between the agrarian conservatives and Mussolini, who had worked out a temporary truce with the Socialist unions during the summer of 1921—the so-called Pacification Pact. Both the cease-fire with the Socialists and the old republican, anticlerical, and radical program of 1919 were scrapped in favor of a free-enterprise, monarchical platform which was designed to appeal to middle-class opinion. The loose movement of 1920 was transformed at this congress into the *Partito Nazionale Fascista*, the National Fascist Party (PNF), with a clearly conservative political orientation.

The Disintegration of the Liberal State

By 1922 the control exercised by the political class through the mechanism of parliament had been so weakened that no one seriously believed that the old system could survive without alteration. Mussolini's asset in 1922 was the widespread belief on the part of many liberals that fascism was an inevitable, if temporary, corrective for a system gone awry. Once this attitude penetrated government deeply enough, the whole mechanism of the state bureaucracy was compromised. Few prefects or police officials were willing to risk their careers to enforce the laws. Those who did, like Cesare Mori of Bologna, reported that they could barely command their subordinates. Prime ministers Ivanoe Bonomi and Luigi Facta, Giolitti's successors, lacked will and authority. Facta, especially, was regarded as merely a stand-in for Giolitti during his two governments from February to October 1922. Former prime ministers Orlando, Nitti, Salandra, and Giolitti sought to return to power by striking a deal with Mussolini. When the actual crisis in government leading to the installation of a Fascist government began, it became difficult for political leaders to use force to prevent something which most had already accepted as inevitable. With the possible exceptions of Giolitti and Nitti, no major figure was ready to govern against the Fascists.

Nor was Italy's social and economic elite hostile to an understanding with fascism. In early October the leaders of the Confindustria made it clear that they supported a Giolitti-Mussolini combination. Mussolini himself worked to ease lingering doubts by repeated assurances that a Fascist government would attempt no radical economic experiments. Mussolini gave similar assurances to the monarchy in a speech in Udine on September 29. The attitude of the army was dependent upon that of the king, but the Fascists had taken every opportunity throughout 1922 to exhibit a promilitary orientation. Not only did former officers figure prominently in the Fascist movement, but Italy's two most important military leaders, Marshalls Armando Diaz and Pietro Badoglio, informed the king on October 7 that the army was favorable to the Fascists. The Catholic Church was similarly well disposed, for on the crucial issue of support for Catholic private schools, the Fascists had responded favorably.

The March on Rome: October 27–29, 1922

The Fascist seizure of power, like its Nazi counterpart in 1933, was not a military conquest or a revolutionary victory. Even the later myth that fascism somehow saved Italy from revolution was untrue. By 1922 the Socialist party had become so divided and weakened that it could no longer mount a threat to the state. Fascism's role, rather than simply to defeat the Socialists, was to create a new framework that would deprive the workers, their party, and the unions of the power to threaten bourgeois Italy at any future time.

The March on Rome was an exercise in psychological warfare, a high-stakes political poker game in which each player attempted to bluff his opponents into submission. The situation was further complicated by the fact that the major protagonists were scattered throughout Italy: Mussolini in Milan, Giolitti at his home in Piedmont, the king at his country estate near Pisa and then in Rome, and the prime minister Facta and the conservative leader Antonio Salandra in Rome. Giolitti's strongest card was his long experience and the support of many industrial leaders who looked with favor on a Giolitti-Mussolini government. Salandra enjoyed the support of the king and of many conservative Fascists who considered him the most acceptable leader of a coalition government. Mussolini enjoyed the certainty that no leader, with the exception of Giolitti, even considered governing against the Fascists.

The campaign of psychological warfare began at the Fascist party congress on October 24 in Naples. Secret plans were laid for a mobilization of the Fascist squads and for the seizure of public buildings and rail centers in the major cities. From there three Fascist columns would converge on Rome. Overall command was entrusted to Michele Bianchi, Italo Balbo, Cesare Maria De Vecchi, and Emilio De Bono. The March on Rome was a calculated risk because the poorly armed Fascists were no match for the regular troops guarding the capital. The aim, however, was to bluff the government into submission.

The crisis in the Facta government formally began when the conservative leader Salandra, hoping to profit from the Fascist maneuvers to arrive in power himself, withdrew his support from the government on October 27. Almost simultaneously, news of the Fascist mobilization arrived in Rome. Pushed by the antifascists in his government, Facta refused to be intimidated. Victor Emmanuel III, who arrived in Rome that evening, agreed in principle to the proclamation of martial law, which would have allowed the government to use troops against the squads. After hectic consultations with his colleagues in the government, an exhausted Facta presented the decree to the king on the morning of October 28. To his dismay, he found that the king had changed his mind and would not sign. The government then resigned.

Three considerations seem to have dictated the royal about-face. The military restated its position that, while it would obey orders, it would prefer not to be put to the test. The king thought that Salandra would form the next government with Mussolini's participation. (He was probably persuaded of this by the Nationalist Luigi Federzoni and the conservative Fascists De Vecchi and Grandi.) Finally, Victor Emmanuel felt that it would be absurd to use force to stop Fascist participation in the government when all leading politicians were agreed on its necessity.

On October 28 Salandra received the mandate to form a government and began frantic negotiations with the Fascists in Rome and a series of fruitless telephone calls to Mussolini in Milan. Mussolini now held all the cards. Salandra had blocked Giolitti, and the conservatives had persuaded the king not to proclaim martial law. Buoyed by support from Milan's industrial elite, Mussolini proceeded to derail Salandra simply by refusing to participate in any government which he did not head. A stunned Salandra abandoned the effort, and on October 29, Benito Mussolini, at age thirty-nine, became Italy's youngest prime minister. Only then did the columns of blackshirts "conquer" Rome.

Part Two
*The Fascist Regime
in Ascendancy
1922–35*

Chapter Three
*Between Movement
and Regime
1922–25*

A Fragile Victory

The success of the Fascist movement in combining violence and political maneuver to complete a semiconstitutional seizure of power was unprecedented in Europe and offered at first no indications for the future. From 1922 to 1925, the Italian political system remained in limbo, a hybrid of authoritarian practice grafted onto the old liberal constitutional forms. Only one thing seemed clear. Once in power, Mussolini announced that he did not intend to leave office voluntarily. The major difficulty that he faced was to balance two conflicting pressures put on his new government. The leaders of the provincial Fascist squads wanted a more thoroughgoing victory than had been achieved by the investiture of the king. Industry, the landowners, the Catholic Church, and the military demanded a period of tranquility after years of tension. These conflicting demands were hard to reconcile, coming, as they did, from groups which Mussolini could not easily afford to offend.

The March on Rome was an ambiguous victory in another sense. The government rested on a solid parliamentary majority of which the Fascists made up only a small part. The balance came from partners in the coalition which Mussolini put together in the days after October 29. Apart from Mussolini himself, who held the post of prime minister and minister of the interior, there were three Fascists, two Catholics, one Liberal, one independent (the philosopher Giovanni Gentile as minister of public instruction), one Nationalist (Luigi Federzoni as colonial minister), two military figures, and two members of a small, southern-based party. Mussolini had even intended to include a representative of the General Confederation of Labor but was forced to yield to pressure from the conservatives.

Mussolini's ultimate aim until January 3, 1925, was to make his government stable within the existing constitutional system, but three forces interacted to defeat this scheme: Mussolini's own authoritarian conception of power, pressure from within the Fascist movement, and resistance from the liberal, democratic, and socialist opposition to unconstitutional violence and repression.

Mussolini as Prime Minister

Mussolini was an extraordinary political tactician, but his skill at maneuver was due in part to the absence of any ethical foundation or any overall political vision. Every individual or institution became an instrument to be used only as long as it served his immediate purpose. Unlike Adolf Hitler, Mussolini was not mentally unbalanced. He operated on the level of ordinary calculation and rationality. In his case, however, the myth of his own indispensability corroded and corrupted to the point that during the 1930s he had to be consulted when the Roman traffic police wanted to wear summer uniforms earlier than usual. Thousands of memos, even the most trivial, crossed his desk to be disposed of with a large "M" scrawled in the margin. As time went on, the myth of the Duce grew larger than the man. All separation between Mussolini's immediate interests and those of Italy disappeared. Initially, his tactical brilliance gave Mussolini an edge over all his rivals, who failed to understand how drastically the rules of the political game had been altered by World War I. In the long run, opportunism became the rule, and debates over policy and ideology lost vigor. Mussolini lacked any corrective to his impulsive, violent, and often fatalistic, nature. A personal myth became a substitute for serious consideration of ends and means.

The Nature of the Fascist Party: A New Elite for a New Italy?

The Fascist party was one propelling force which carried Italy toward dictatorship. By 1923 it was already quite different from the party of 1921 and light years away from the group of outsiders who had met in March 1919. Actually, there were three subparties that coexisted uncomfortably: the provincial Fascist leaders and their squads; conservative landowners and businessmen, who joined the movement as it rose to power; and younger, urban, technocratic Fascists, who joined the movement as a way of altering the political and social system. Allied to the party were large numbers of conservative fellow travelers (businessmen, professionals, Catholics), who waited to cast their lot with the Fascists until the movement gave specific guarantees as to its future conduct.

The provincial *squadristi* were discontented with the outcome of the March on Rome. The compromise with the old conservative establishment threatened to thwart their aspirations for further political advancement. Mussolini only partially controlled this provincial movement whose base of strength lay in the armed squads of a given province. Much of northern and central Italy was divided into little principalities under the local Fascist chiefs or ras, who used their power to carry out policies that were often at variance with the national leadership. Roberto Farinacci of Cremona was the unofficial leader of the provincial intransigents, but he was one of many: Cesare Maria De Vecchi in Turin, Carlo Scorza in Lucca, Leandro Arpinati, Dino Grandi, and Gino Baroncini in Bologna, Renato Ricci in Massa Carrara, Italo Balbo in Ferrara, Antonio Arrivabene and Giuseppe Moschini in Mantua. The most powerful of the ras were aided in their independence by the fact that money for the squads came not from the national party but from the local agrarian and industrial groups. Some of the ras even controlled newspapers of national significance, like Farinacci's *Cremona Nuova* and Balbo's *Corriere Padano*. Provincial leaders like Farinacci pushed for a more radical break with the constitutional system than did fascism's other constituencies (monarchy, army, industry, Vatican), who called for normalization and were offended by the orgy of violence on the part of the victorious Fascists. This post-March violence reached a climax on December 18, 1922, in Turin, when eighteen workers were murdered in unprovoked attacks by De Vecchi's Fascist squads. Mussolini needed the squads as a weapon against both allies and opponents, but he wished to reduce them to a docile instrument in the service of his own power. Throughout the years from 1923 to 1926, Mussolini maneuvered to accomplish this aim. In December 1922 and January 1923, two important measures were taken to increase his control over the party—the creation of the Voluntary Militia for National Security (MVSN), which was designed to bring the squads under a central command, and the institution of the Fascist Grand Council as the main policy-making body for the party. In the short run, neither the militia nor the Grand Council served its purpose. Instead, the legalization of a private army caused friction with the opposition and worried the military leaders. The Grand Council, which was to have gathered all factions of the movement under Mussolini's watchful eye, was seen by his coalition partners as a sort of parallel government and did little to tame the restive provincial ras. (It did play an important role in the later constitutional development of the regime when it acted as a link between party and state.)

The most successful way of dealing with the provincials involved not institutional controls but a long-range campaign of undermining their influence. This came about in some cases by co-option. Italo Balbo and Dino Grandi preferred recognition and high position in Rome. De Vecchi was moved from Turin to the governorship of Somalia. The leader of Neapolitan fascism, Aurelio Padovani, was a more difficult case. Padovani had attempted to build the local party outside of traditional political clienteles. When such ambitions conflicted with the wishes of fascism's new conservative southern political allies, Padovani became an embarrassment to be shunted aside. Unlike Balbo or Grandi, he refused offers of employment elsewhere and left the party. Another way Mussolini undermined the power of the local ras was by breaking their ties to the provincial political and economic establishment. This happened in Bologna, when Gino Baroncini was undercut by the prefect Arturo Bocchini until he could be replaced by the more obliging Arpinati. Over the long run, the struggle for control of the ras could be won only when the opposition was totally suppressed. Until then, their political function was too vital to be dispensed with.

The second faction of the PNF was composed of conservatives who swarmed to the party just before and after the March on Rome. Many of these were landowners and professionals from the South where the Fascist party had never been strong. In certain areas, like Tuscany, elements of the old aristocracy also joined the movement. Further powerful reinforcements for the conservatives came through the fusion of the PNF with the Italian Nationalist Association in March 1923, which brought to fascism a number of highly intelligent leaders like Luigi Federzoni and Alfredo Rocco, who were to play key roles in subordinating the Fascist party to the traditional state bureaucracy.

The third component of the movement was made up of middle-class professionals who advocated technocratic modernization and spread their views in journals like Giuseppe Bottai's *Critica Fascista*. Their model was government by the best talents of the wartime generation. They wanted to transform the PNF into a select party by purging its more violent members and by recruiting among university-trained professionals. Bottai and Massimo Rocca, a former anarcho-syndicalist-turned-Nationalist and monarchist, mounted in late 1923 what came to be known as the "revisionist" campaign against the provincial extremists. At times, Mussolini would use these techno-cratic elitists in his battle against the provincial squadrists, but he was in no way committed to their technocratic outlook.

Conservative Allies of Fascism: The Fellow Travelers

The liberal and Catholic partners in Mussolini's government presented radically different problems for his consolidation of power. The liber-als, who finally gave themselves a formal party organization in October 1922, remained divided among followers of Giolitti, Salandra, and Giovanni Amendola, an antifascist who would be one of the victims of Fascist repression in 1926. Faced with the defection to the PNF of their local clienteles, most old-line liberals preferred Giolitti's strategy of waiting until Mussolini made a major mistake before reasserting their control.

The Catholic Popular party presented an entirely different problem. Its mass base still existed, and Luigi Sturzo, the party secretary, was determined to maintain the independence of the PPI. The crisis in Mussolini's relationship with the *Popolari* came in early 1923, when the government introduced a project for electoral reform, known as the Acerbo law (after its Fascist sponsor, Giacomo Acerbo). This law kept proportional representation but gave two-thirds of the seats in parliament to the party or electoral list that gained a plurality of at least 25 percent of the total vote. The other third would be divided among the opposition parties and lists. Most conservatives justified the reform as a way of reducing the power of the left and of ensuring strong government, but the fate of the bill depended on the Catholics. With the Socialists, Communists, and Liberal Democrats opposed to the Acerbo Law, the Popular party would have to support the legislation or abstain. Mussolini acted to undermine the PPI's leadership by coming to a direct understanding with the Vatican. When the congress of the Popular party affirmed its independence of ministerial discipline in April 1923, Mussolini dropped its members from the government. Finally, in June 1923, he managed to persuade the Vatican to abandon Sturzo, who had little choice but to resign as secretary of the party. Without its founder and political secretary, and faced with constant attacks from the squads, the *Popolari* broke ranks. Many abstained, or voted for the Acerbo Law, which was passed on July 21 by a vote of 223 to 123.

Dominant Interest Groups and the New Fascist Government

The Vatican. The first step toward an understanding between Mussolini's government and the Vatican came after a meeting on January 20, 1923, between Mussolini and Cardinal Pietro Gasparri, the Vatican secretary of state, at which the Italian government agreed to bail out the Church-controlled Bank of Rome. Other gestures followed. The Fascist party in February 1923 forbade membership in freemasonic organizations. The Catholic catechism was introduced in elementary schools and the crucifix in schools and state offices. This success in dealing with the government directly convinced the Vatican, which disliked the independence of the Popular party, to shift its support to the more malleable Catholic Action organization, which was directly under the control of the local bishop.

Industry. The March on Rome caught the major figures of Italian industry in Giolitti's camp, although they rapidly switched sides on October 28. Once in power, the Fascists profited from the European recovery of 1922–25. The index of industrial production (1938 = 100) rose from 54 in 1921 to 83 in 1925. Production in all major sectors rose dramatically, while unemployment decreased by 72 percent. The power balance shifted completely from the workers to management. Days lost in strikes declined from 18 million in 1919 and 16 million in 1920 to just under 300,000 in 1923. Membership in the General Confederation of Labor dropped from its peak of 2.5 million in 1920 to under 500,000 in 1923.

The first measures of the Mussolini government were designed to please industry. Alberto De Stefani, a convinced economic liberal, became the new finance minister. He reduced controls over industry and cut expenditures and taxes. On December 3, 1922, the government was granted power to reform the tax laws and to trim the bureaucracy by decree. Other moves quickly followed: the investigation into war profits and the publication of stock ownership were dropped; telephone companies were restored to private control; the concessions given to electrical companies were renewed; the state monopoly over life insurance companies was ended.

While not totally committed to the Fascist government, the industrialists were impressed by the willingness of Mussolini to meet their demands in two vital areas: the suppression of agitation from the working class and minimal interference by the government in the way large firms regulated their own affairs. Although some important industrial spokesmen, like Gino Olivetti, the secretary-general of the Confindustria, were skeptical about the new government, most considered it the best possible solution.

Mussolini understood this opposition to intervention in industrial affairs by the Fascist party or unions. He purchased support in the business community by allowing heavy industry to establish its own fiefdom within the regime. A first indication of the direction that the Fascist government would take came on December 19, 1923, when the leaders of the Confindustria and the Fascist Syndical Confederation signed the Palazzo Chigi Accords. The industrialists promised exclusive bargaining rights to the Fascist unions in return for abandonment by the Fascist syndicates of any projects for integral corporativism, i.e. the inclusion of employers and workers within a single organization. In practice, the industrialists continued to negotiate with the weakened nonfascist unions whenever they represented a significant number of workers, but they thwarted any social experimentation on the part of the Fascist unions or the regime.

Agriculture. Perhaps no group was as clearly identified with fascism as were the agrarians of the Po Valley, but much of their support went to the local ras rather than to the national coffers. Moreover, the agrarians were slow to form an effective national organization on the model of the cohesive Confindustria. The agrarians, however, achieved four immediate aims from the triumph of fascism. First, there was the destruction of the peasant leagues. Between November 1921 and October 1922, thirty-seven strikes, involving 43,000 workers took place in agriculture. The next year hardly any strike activity was reported. The balance shifted so dramatically that even the Fascists complained that the landowners were refusing to respect contracts signed with the Fascist peasant unions. With the destruction of the peasant leagues all guarantees of employment and wage levels could be (and were) violated. Second, the Visocchi decree of 1920, regulating the occupation of land by peasants, was revoked. Third, the landowners received a modification of inheritance taxes and a substantial easing of taxation on profits from large-scale agriculture. Finally, the forced resignation of the local Socialist administrations restored landlord control over Italy's towns and villages. Most of these gains accrued to the largest and most powerful of the agrarians, while the small farmers benefited only indirectly.

King and Army. A unique feature of the Fascist regime throughout its twenty-year history was the coexistence of the monarchy with Fascist institutions. The king continued to represent a link with the prefascist past and to hold strong loyalties in the army, the state bureaucracy, and the senate. Certainly Mussolini owed much to the king. In October 1922, Victor Emmanuel's decision determined how Mussolini would come to power. Thereafter, until 1925, the king sought a strong government that would remain within the limits of the constitutional system. The attitude of the monarch paralleled that of the army. Mussolini's appointment of Marshall Armando Diaz, the commander-in-chief at the end of the war, as his first war minister further instilled confidence. Minor problems arose over the Fascist militia, but neither Mussolini nor the army had any interest in seeing it develop into a real power center. In general, Mussolini showed himself more than willing to offer the military its autonomous sphere within the structure of the regime.

Fascism and the Middle Class

If fascism had a mass constituency, it was the middle class, which had been subjected to intense social and economic pressure in the postwar era. For better or worse, fascism became the political movement through which a substantial number of students, professionals, small businessmen, landowners, and shopkeepers sought to achieve their aims.

Foremost among the difficulties to be resolved by the new government was the oversupply of intellectuals and white-collar professionals. The minister of public instruction Giovanni Gentile complained that thousands of teachers and other professionals were graduated each year with no hope of finding employment. Professional organizations looked to the Fascist government for relief, which eventually took two forms. First, the Fascists worked to favor veterans and to discriminate against women in the highly competitive white-collar market. Second, by the introduction of the Gentile Education Reform of 1923 the government sought to reduce the number of students moving into the employment market. More precisely, Gentile's reform had the effect of reducing the number of students in the secondary schools from 337,000 in 1923, to 237,000 in 1926–27. The number of university students also dropped, from 53,000 in 1919–20, to 40,000 in 1928–29. The new government reduced aid to smaller and weaker universities, reorganized technical education by providing minimal technical skills for the mass of students in schools that would not lead to higher levels of education, and introduced rigid state examinations at the end of the cycle of secondary education. There was a notable drop in enrollment in the *scuola tecnica* (technical high school), which had been a major avenue for advancement because it provided both a degree of general technical education and the possibility of further educational opportunity. When the *scuola tecnica* was replaced by the *scuola complementare*, which was closed to higher educational advancement, most students

stopped attending. Thus, by looking at both the expansion and con-
traction in enrollment in the *scuola tecnica*, one can see the opportunity
for social mobility at the end of World War I and the efforts of the
Fascists to close the door:

1900–1901	38,324
1920–21	133,442
1922–23	112,981
1923–24	65,123

Over the long run, apart from efforts to stabilize the labor market,
fascism offered a number of tangible benefits to the middle class, such
as employment in state and party bureaucracies, protection for small
businesses through licencing restrictions, veterans' preferences, and
increased differentials between blue- and white-collar wages. Largely
excluded from these gains, however, were middle-class women,
whose status had improved during the war and immediate postwar
period, and who had expected further gains in the form of voting rights
and the removal of discriminatory laws in the exercise of professions.

The Opposition

The opposition to fascism in 1923 and 1924 was composed of Giovanni
Amendola's Liberal Democrats on the right; various reformist
socialists, now organized in the Unitary Socialist party, some Republicans, and the *Popolari* in the center; and the Italian Socialist party and
the Communist party of Italy on the left. These factions and parties
were so badly split that they offered little hope of a coherent alternative.
In 1923 Mussolini attempted to weaken further any potential antifascist
front by separating the Italian Confederation of Labor from the rest of
the opposition. Such a move would not only have dealt a crippling
blow to the Socialists, but would have gained for the Fascists an
infrastructure which would have linked the government to the masses
without the bother of constructing a Fascist labor organization. Much
depended on the outcome of the elections, scheduled by Mussolini for
early 1924 in the hope of finally stabilizing his power.

The Elections of 1924

The elections of April 6, 1924, marked the final stage in a long effort to consolidate the power of the Fascist government within the framework of the existing institutions. Mussolini hoped that elections under the Acerbo law would allow him to govern from a secure base. To ensure his victory, Mussolini sponsored a "national list," which included a large number of nonfascist liberals, like Orlando and Salandra, and Catholic conservatives who had broken with the Popular party. Only Nitti, who did not run, and Giolitti, who fielded his own list in Piedmont, refused to take part.

The results gave the government list 66 percent of the votes and 374 of 535 seats in the new parliament. But the victory was tainted by widespread violence and fraud. In rural areas, where Fascist terror reigned, the term "free elections" became a mockery. Moreover, the victory was less overwhelming by regional breakdown. The Fascists won only 54.3 percent of the vote in the North but piled up 81 percent in the South. If Emilia, where Fascist squads worked overtime on election day, is excluded, the opposition parties probably carried the politically advanced North in the face of tremendous odds.

Taken as a whole, the elections marked a major turnover in the political class. Almost everywhere, the old liberal political establishment did poorly. Salandra was elected in fourteenth place in 1924, whereas he led the ticket in 1921. The average age of the Fascist deputy was thirty-seven, whereas their conservative allies averaged forty-eight years. Eighty percent of the Fascist deputies were new to parliament, and two-thirds were under forty. In short, fascism attempted, in the election of 1924, to pay its debt to the war generation by working a substantial change in political personnel.

The elections also helped to consolidate the alliance between the Fascist government and industrial and financial elite groups. The Association of Italian Joint Stock Companies set up a percentage levy on its members for the Fascist electoral fund, and several prominent industrialists ran for parliament on the National List.

The Matteotti Murder and the Crisis of Fascist Power

The elections of April 1924 brought Mussolini a victory at the price of increasing the conservative pressures on his government. However, the elections revealed that fascism had yet to establish links with the mass of organized workers in the North. The Fascists had not been able to dislodge the Socialists and Communists from their positions as leaders of the industrial workers. Fascism had to accomplish this goal before its claim to political supremacy would be secure.

Such considerations led Mussolini to renew his courtship of the General Confederation of Labor following the elections of 1924. Opposition to these overtures for the inclusion of labor representatives in the government came not only from the ras and the Fascist unions but also from the leadership of the Socialist opposition, which resisted blurring the moral line between the Fascists and the democratic opposition. Ironically, the most forthright of the moral resisters was Giacomo Matteotti, secretary of the Unitary Socialist party, from whose ranks came the labor leaders most interested in striking a deal with Mussolini.

Matteotti was one of the most talented of the younger generation of socialists. Born in 1885, the son of a land-owning family of the Po Valley, he was drawn to socialism while still a law student. His socialism was of the pragmatic, nonrevolutionary variety, and, from the beginning, Matteotti was a natural opponent of the flamboyant Mussolini. He had always considered fascism to be a moral question and had amassed much material proving electoral fraud and perhaps even financial misconduct on the part of the Fascists. Matteotti courageously used this ammunition to attack the legality of the elections in a blistering speech to parliament on May 30, 1924. An angry Mussolini made it clear that he wanted Matteotti punished. On June 10 the Socialist leader disappeared. Although the body was not found until August, there was no doubt that Matteotti had been murdered by the Fascists.

The Matteotti crisis had three repercussions. First, it opened a chasm between the regime and its opposition and ended any chance of normalization within the framework of the constitution. Second, the murder strengthened the influence of the conservatives, who now saw an opportunity to exact recognition of their spheres of influence from a weakened Mussolini. Finally, the crisis gave new life to the provincial extremists, who demanded harsh measures against the opposition, but set up a long-term confrontation between conservative and extreme wings of fascism.

Despite doubts that Mussolini had actually ordered Matteotti's murder, evidence of his moral and political responsibility was overwhelming. He created the special squads which administered punitive lessons to prominent opposition leaders, like the liberals Giovanni Amendola and Piero Gobetti, or the communist Francesco Misiano. Evidence of the order to attack Matteotti was traced to Mussolini's immediate entourage. His close aides Cesare Rossi and Aldo Finzi were involved in the murder and the cover-up.

The death of Matteotti almost toppled Mussolini's government. Danger came from two directions. On June 13 an outraged antifascist opposition, composed of Liberal Democrats, Catholics, Socialists, Republicans, and Communists, withdrew from parliament until the government resigned. The moderate leadership of this so-called Aventine Secession rejected Communist party calls for a general strike and instead opted for an appeal to the king to dismiss Mussolini. This strict legalitarian approach presupposed, however, that the opposition could offer an alternative that would reassure the conservatives. The second danger to Mussolini was more insidious because it came from elements within and allied to his parliamentary majority. The antifascists gambled that mounting evidence of Fascist guilt would convince these conservatives that the government had to be replaced. Instead, the dominant interests became more wary about the opposition and pressed to increase their power within the framework of the Fascist government. Direct power continued to frighten the conservatives, who would then have to deal with both the Fascist squads and the Socialist and Communist party masses. They had no assurance how rapidly the fortunes of the extreme left would revive, once the pressure of fascism was removed. It was much safer to work with a crippled Mussolini. The demands of the conservative right were presented by Luigi Federzoni, the former leader of the Italian Nationalist Association. The results were announced on June 16: a purge of Mussolini's aides, the appointment of Federzoni to the Interior Ministry, and the nomination of a number of liberals, Catholics, and Nationalists to government posts.

The formation of the Mussolini-Federzoni government had the desired effect. The king made no move to remove Mussolini. The military merely used the crisis to press for further controls over the Fascist militia. The Catholic Church acted effectively to support the Mussolini government by a papal warning on September 8 against collaboration between Socialists and Catholics. Similarly, the industrialists sought to increase their influence rather than pass into opposition.

The remote possibility that the conservatives might defect from the Fascist coalition did not entirely vanish until December 1924. In fact, during November and December several attempts were made to bring the Aventine opposition together with Giolitti or Salandra, who had belatedly taken a stand against the government. In the end, the majority of conservatives, led by Federzoni, stood firm in support of fascism. By the end of December, Mussolini was able to yield to the demands of the Fascist extremists for decisive action against the opposition. Backed by the Fascist party and by the conservatives, Mussolini in a defiant speech to parliament on January 3, 1925, challenged his opponents to remove him.

The "Long Voyage" Through Fascism Begins: The Repression

While Mussolini's declaration did not turn Italy into a complete dictatorship overnight, it marked the beginning of a process that eventually led to the creation of a new, authoritarian political and constitutional order. Compared to what took place in Nazi Germany a decade later, the Fascists were relatively slow in consolidating their power. Moreover, repression did not augment the role of the Fascist party, but rather reduced its political independence and initiative. The dictatorship was instituted within the structure of the traditional state. Repression in Italy was also quite selective. It bore hardest on the politicized workers and peasants and on the intermediate elite groups who had defected to the revolutionary camp, but it allowed substantial autonomy to the various conservative fiefdoms. Industry, the military, the Church, even the universities, continued, to a large degree, to manage their own affairs.

The impact of Mussolini's new hard line was felt immediately by the opposition. Federzoni issued instructions to the prefects on January 5,

1925, to enforce rigorously the press laws of July 1923, which allowed the government to suspend publications deemed to have preached class hatred or disrespect for the monarchy, the Catholic Church, or the state.

The new institutional framework was created in 1925 and 1926. The first series of laws were enacted after an attempt on Mussolini's life on November 4, 1925, by Tito Zaniboni, a Social Democratic deputy. The cornerstone of legislative repression followed in the form of the "Law on the Powers of the Head of Government" of December 1925, which ended parliamentary control over the government by making the prime minister responsible only to the king. In November and December other laws were passed against secret societies, ostensibly aimed at the freemasons, but in fact designed to purge the bureaucracy. The Unitary Socialist party, to which Zaniboni belonged, was banned as a first step in the suppression of all opposition parties. In February and September 1926, elected local governments were replaced by appointed officials, the *podestà*. In this way the government paid off a debt to the agrarians, who regained complete control over local affairs.

A second wave of repressive legislation followed in 1926 after three more attempts on Mussolini's life. The first assassination effort was by Violet Gibson, a disturbed Anglo-Irish woman, on April 7, 1926; the second, on September 11, by the anarchist Gino Lucetti, led to the installation of a tough former prefect and bureaucratic traditionalist, Arturo Bocchini, as head of the state police; the third, on October 31, was attributed to an obscure young Bolognese, Anteo Zamboni, but possibly was made by the Fascists themselves in order to provoke the final break with the past. The cumulative effect of these attempts was far reaching. The conservative Federzoni lost his position as interior minister to Mussolini (who never again relinquished it). The significance of this move was lessened, however, because the work of reinforcing the state against control by the Fascist party had already been completed. On November 6, 1926, a new police law gave to the government extensive powers of confinement for both common and political crimes and extended the government's power to dissolve political and cultural associations. Three days later, on November 9, the opposition members of parliament lost their seats. In December 1926, the "Law for the Defense of the State" was passed. It introduced a penalty of death for attempts on the lives of members of the government and royal family and established a separate court for political trials, the Special Tribunal, and the secret police, the OVRA. Much of the repressive legislation was the work of the former Nationalists Luigi Federzoni and Alfredo Rocco. Rocco, the legal architect of the regime, was appointed minister of justice on January 12, 1925, and held the post until July 1932. Both of these statist conservatives opposed increased influence for the Fascist party. They allowed no counterpart in Italy to the German SS. Even the political police were controlled by career bureaucrats, like Arturo Bocchini, who remained chief of state security until his death in 1940, and Carmine Senise, who held the post until early 1943.

By the end of 1926 the political opposition was outlawed, except for a handful of liberal senators and deputies. The remaining democratic unions were suppressed in 1926. Only the Communist party maintained a small, but active, clandestine apparatus within Italy, but it was periodically decimated by police raids. The Socialist and Liberal Democratic parties slowly and painfully reconstituted themselves in France after 1926.

In 1927 the Fascists were able to force the resignations of many high-level bureaucrats in the civil service and the diplomatic corps. They were replaced by Fascists, the so-called class of '27 in the Foreign Ministry, who gave a more distinct Fascist coloring to policy. Yet this infusion of Fascists into the bureaucracy was no measure of progress toward achieving a totalitarian state or even of gaining party control of the state. Despite purges, the old structures and mentalities survived; Fascists merely became part of the existing system. A striking example of this phenomenon was the appointment of Dino Grandi as undersecretary at the Interior Ministry to watch over the Nationalist Federzoni. Grandi rapidly adjusted to Federzoni's conservative policies and continued to become more establishment oriented when he shifted to the Foreign Ministry in 1927. Similarly, in the legal profession and the universities Fascists singled out only their most vocal opponents for punishment, without touching basic structures.

Only journalism was especially hard hit by the repression. In November 1925, Luigi Albertini, the liberal editor of Milan's *Corriere della Sera* and Italy's most respected journalist, was removed along with a large part of his staff. Ownership of Italy's second most important paper, *La Stampa* of Turin, passed to the Fiat auto firm, which appointed a Fascist editor. *L'Avanti!*, *L'Unità* (the Communist daily), *La Voce Repubblicana*, and the liberal weekly *Il Mondo* were suppressed in 1926. That same year saw changes at the top of all important papers. In February 1928 journalists were required to register in the professional directory of the Fascist Journalists' Association. In contrast, bastions of the conservative economic establishment, like the Confindustria, merely tacked the term "Fascist" on the title with no changes in their internal structure or personnel.

Chapter Four
*The Creation of
the Regime
1926–29*

During the years from 1926 until 1935, Italian fascism reached the high point of its power and prestige in Italy and abroad. This longer period can be divided into subperiods: 1926–29, when the Fascist government institutionalized its working relationship with the major independent power centers of Italy; 1929–35, when the regime grappled with the consequences of the depression, launched its corporative experiments, and moved to create a new relationship with the masses.

Economic Policy and Industrial Development: An Overview

Although elements of Fascist economic policy were evident as early as 1922, the distinctive features emerged only in 1925 with the abandonment of De Stefani's liberal economic orientation. Two difficulties arise in evaluating Fascist economic policy and performance. First, what was distinctively Fascist must be distinguished from the general development of capitalist economies between 1922 and 1939. Many industrialized nations attempted similar regulatory and protectionist policies during the Interwar Period. Second, in portraying Fascist economic development in terms of growth or stagnation, only an analysis by sector and by impact on social groups can give an idea of what really happened. Sweeping negative judgments are hard to sustain for the simple reason that burdens fell with extraordinary inequality on different sectors and social groups.

What were the features of the Italian economy during the Fascist era?

Fascism favored heavy, or basic, industry, like steel, electricity, and chemicals, over light or consumer-oriented industry. Weak consumer demand was perpetuated by a deliberate policy of low wages. The entire period was marked by a process of consolidation, cartelization, and rationalization within industry. During the 1930s this process took place behind the facade of the corporative system. Agriculture continued to lose ground in relation to industry despite the government's ruralization campaigns. Employment in the favored heavy industry grew more slowly than the work force, which led to much underemployment, which was hidden in the bloated service and agricultural sectors and in the state bureaucracy. The Fascist regime increased the public sector through a major reorganization and expansion of state agencies. An increasingly close relationship between the private and public sectors developed. The cornerstone of the new mixed system was the Istituto per la Ricostruzione Industriale (IRI), created in 1933 as a giant holding company for state participation in heavy industry. State institutions took the place of private banks as the source of long-term industrial credit, and a unique system of parastate agencies was created. Though formally public, these agencies acted within the structure of capitalist enterprise.

The Reorganization of the Fascist Economy: Relations with Industry, 1926–29

Although rapid economic growth from 1922 to 1925 helped initially to cement relations with industry, there were signs by 1925 that expansion was bringing unwanted strains into the economic and social system. Inflation weakened the lira on foreign markets and had a negative impact on the fixed-income middle class. Rapid growth also furthered the development of the urban proletariat, which remained a source of opposition to the regime. Finally, the failure to control inflation threatened to upset the financial and industrial backers of the regime.

While it would be an error to speak of a basic clash of interests between the industrial community and fascism, a number of problems developed around 1925. The first involved the spillover effect of the

Matteotti crisis. During the crisis, several important industrialists had come close to defecting from support for Mussolini's government. A second, related, problem emerged. One of the weapons used by Mussolini to intimidate the fellow travelers in industry was to allow more freedom to the Fascist unions. The number of strikes increased from 200 in 1923 to 355 in 1924, and in early 1925 there was even a Fascist-led strike in Brescia. The industrialists disliked this agitation, which took on more ominous overtones as the Fascist unions again pressed for a monopoly of labor representation. The industrial employers continued to prefer to deal with a number of small, weak unions. Finally, the industrial-financial community became increasingly preoccupied by the decline of the lira on the international markets.

Mussolini moved rapidly to ease the accumulating tension. On July 8, 1925, De Stefani was replaced as finance minister by Giuseppe Volpi, a banker and industrialist. Giuseppe Belluzzo, a former Nationalist with ties to heavy industry, replaced Cesare Nava as minister of national economy. Belluzzo and Volpi moved aggressively to balance the budget, to ease pressure on the balance of payments by a deflationary policy, to gain the support of foreign (mainly American) capital for the consolidation of the Italian debt, and to introduce increased tariff protection for agriculture and industry.

As part of the effort to improve the climate between industry and the government, Mussolini in July instructed the prefects, who were in charge of civil and police administration in a given province, to put an end to labor agitation. He then brought the Confindustria and the Fascist Syndical Confederation together by the Palazzo Vidoni Accord of October 2, 1925. The agreement minimized the danger to the industrialists of a Fascist labor monopoly. Two major concessions were exchanged. The industrialists won from the unions the suppression of the internal commissions and of shop representatives, thereby cutting the unions off from direct supervision of national contracts on the plant level. In return, the industrialists conceded the inevitable exclusive bargaining rights to the Fascist unions.

The Quota 90

The most controversial measure undertaken by the government before

1929 was the revaluation of the lira, or the *quota 90* (an exchange rate of ninety lira to the pound sterling). Revaluation was carried out against the background of a precipitous fall of the lira from 117.5 to the English pound in January 1925, to 138 in June and 144.9 in July, when Italy entered the market to bolster the lira. The rate stabilized until the spring of 1926, when it again shot up to 148 by August.

When Mussolini announced revaluation in a speech at Pesaro on August 18, 1926, he had several objectives in mind. The government wanted to reassure foreign lenders of its ability to control the economy. The Fascists linked their prestige to the status of the lira. Antifascist exile groups pointed to its decline as an indication that the regime was losing the confidence of finance and industry. Mussolini's aims went beyond concern for foreign opinion, however. He sought to reassure those basic constituencies of fascism that were being hurt by continued inflation.

While there was general agreement on the need for a revaluation, there was absolutely no consensus on how far the government should go in its efforts to increase the value of the lira. Between September 1926 and April 1927, the lira rose from 148 to 85 against the pound. When the government finally decided to peg the lira at 90, which was roughly where it stood when Mussolini took power, the decision was far more drastic than anything the bankers and industrialists wanted. Volpi favored a 120 rate, but Mussolini was determined to exert a degree of authority. After initial expressions of concern, industry readily adjusted to the new situation. In fact, the large corporations took advantage of the crisis to eliminate their weaker rivals. The number of mergers in 1928 and 1929 skyrocketed, which only tended to accentuate already strong concentrations of industrial power. By 1932, 144 corporations, .88 percent of the total, held 51.7 percent of all corporate capital.

Rather than marking fundamental changes in Italian economic development, the tariff protection, revaluation, and various public works measures enacted in 1925 and 1926 intensified existing trends by continuing to favor heavy industry. These essentially conservative policies were designed to restrain rapid urbanization and the development of an industrial proletariat and to redress the balance between rural and urban Italy. Controlled expansion and market-sharing accords proved an economically and socially acceptable alternative to rapid growth.

Agriculture and Fascism: An Overview

Fascist agricultural policy can be divided into distinct phases. From 1922 to 1925 there was a prolongation of some postwar trends: continued growth in peasant small holdings, a decline in sharecropping, and increased private investment in mechanization. Most important of all, the power of the peasants to contract on an equal basis was broken during this period.

The following ten years, from 1925 to 1935, marked an extended period of crisis for the agricultural sector. The first and most notable change was the reversal of the trend to peasant proprietorship. Modernization and mechanization also slowed as landlords returned to the less risky and socially more conservative system of sharecropping. These sharecropping arrangements were made in the context of a resurgence of conservative power on the land and were quite favorable to the landlords, who shifted the risk of declining prices onto the sharecropping family. The revival of sharecropping caused further numerical declines in the category of day laborers, who had been the backbone of the Socialist peasant leagues. The accentuation of social differences on the land isolated the radicalized landless proletariat.

Another feature of these depression years was a tragic decline in the rural standard of living, which was reflected in the collapse of agricultural prices. Overall, advanced northern agriculture, which continued its technological progress, profited more from governmental policies than did the South, but there was a steady erosion of the overall position of agriculture with respect to industry in terms of employment, investment, and percentage of national income.

The final period from 1936 to 1939, saw a slight recovery of the agricultural sector from its depression low. These years were marked by increased world demand and by some improvement of agricultural-versus-industrial prices. Within Italy the years immediately preceding World War II saw the integration of agriculture into military planning through state stockpiling and regulation of production.

Population in Agriculture by Type of Landholding or the Equivalent
(in thousands of persons)

	Owner-Operator		Tenant farmers		Sharecroppers		Workers	
	Total	%	Total	%	Total	%	Total	%
1901	2,583	26.9	800	8.3	2,010	20.9	4,188	43.6
1911	1,715	19	727	8.1	1,581	17.5	4,974	55.9
1921	3,427	33.6	696	6.8	1,590	15.6	4,465	43.8
1931	2,990	37	1,000	12.4	1,657	20.5	2,408	29.8
1936	2,930	33.5	1,631	18.6	1,788	20.4	2,379	27.2

SOURCE: Ornello Vitali, *La popolazione attiva in agricoltura attraverso i censimenti italiani* (Rome, 1968), table 1, cited in Jon E. Cohen, "Fascism and Agriculture in Italy: Policies and Consequences," *Economic History Review* 32 (February 1979): 82.

Percentage of National Income

	Agriculture	Industry	Services
1901–10	46.6%	23.4%	30%
1911–20	45.9	28.7	25.4
1921–30	38.2	31.4	30.4
1931–40	29.8	32.8	37.4
1960	19.2	48.2	32.5

SOURCE: Ester Fano Damascelli, "La restaurazione antifascista liberista," *Il movimento di liberazione in Italia* 23 (July–September 1971): 53.

Agriculture and Fascism, 1925–29

The first major undertaking of the Fascist regime in agricultural policy was the "Battle of Grain," announced in 1925. It involved increased tariffs on imported grains to protect Italian wheat producers. The result was a domestic price well above the world market. Despite the high cost, the policy developed out of the basic directives of Fascist political economy. Foremost was the fact that wheat imports added to the deficit in the balance of trade. Volpi and Belluzzo sought to correct this deficit, and self-sufficiency in a major agricultural import was essential. But the logic was not strictly economic. Support for the production of grain in the North rewarded both the large-scale grain farmers of the Po Valley who could afford to mechanize and their industrial suppliers of machinery and fertilizers, major constituencies of the Fascist regime.

The cost of the policy was as great as the advantage but fell on different groups. Expansion of grain production was achieved at the expense of other export-oriented crops (fruits, vegetables, olives) and of livestock production because of the higher cost of fodder. In 1928 Italy lost a half million head of livestock, and the herds continued to decline until 1936. Some of the gains from increased self-sufficiency in wheat were lost in the increased importation of meat and eggs, but there was also a decline in the quality of the average Italian diet. Finally, high tariffs merely protected the inefficient and slowed mechanization outside of the dynamic Po Valley.

The second feature of agricultural policy, ruralization, was announced by Mussolini on May 26, 1927, and represented a shift in orientation for the Fascist regime. The core of early fascism was urban. Mussolini's first base was in Milan, and among his earliest allies were the Futurists, who advocated an urban, industrial destiny for Italy. Mussolini identified with certain aspects of modern technology, like aviation. Even as late as the mid-1920s, the *Popolo d'Italia* urged that Milan become a major European center. This theme abruptly changed in 1927. Henceforth the regime encouraged a return to the land and a high rural birthrate. These policies were designed to reinforce traditional social structures in rural Italy and to overcome what the regime felt was declining national vitality due to the low urban birthrates. The government even issued regulations (largely ignored) in 1927 requiring licenses for the construction of new industry that employed over one hundred workers in population centers of 100,000 or more. This policy flew in the face of Italian social trends. Italians were migrating to the cities from relatively overpopulated rural areas. By encouraging a higher birthrate, the regime added to unemployment and did little to ease the problems of rural Italy.

The third undertaking that directly concerned agriculture during this period was the institution of the *bonifica integrale*, integral land-reclamation program, which was the brainchild of Arrigo Serpieri, a former social democrat turned technocrat. Under the plan, whole areas were to be designated for reclamation projects with the government providing support for a variety of improvements. Serpieri hoped to use the law to attack unproductive land use in the South by including a confiscation clause for owners who failed to use their own capital for improvements, but conservative opposition forced him from office when he tried to apply the provision. Although the policy of land reclamation had some successes, such as the Pontine Marshes, the overall picture was less positive. In part, public investment was merely substituted for private with no provision for forcing landowners to apply new techniques. Only 58 percent of the reclamation projects and 32 percent of the irrigation projects were completed, and only 16 percent were carried through to the *bonifica integrale* state. Moreover, the largest number of projects were in the North and only increased the gap between that area and the South.

Fascist agricultural policy during this period met decidedly mixed results. It helped stabilize the social structure of rural Italy by consolidating agrarian institutions, like the *mezzadria* (sharecropping), despite unfavorable contracts under which landlords determined crops, production, and marketing. Under the Charter of the Mezzadria of 1933, the landowners' gains were consolidated by requirements for a one-year tenancy, abrogation of the requirement of six months' notice for cancellation, and extension of the contract to all members of the tenant's family. The demographic aspect of the ruralization policy was less successful. The census of 1931 revealed that, for the first time, over 50 percent of the population was engaged in nonagricultural pursuits. The percentage living in towns of under one thousand inhabitants dropped in ten years from 54.8 percent to 49.7 percent and increased in towns of over one hundred thousand from 13 to 17 percent, although it can be argued that the losses would have been even greater without the change in policy. Finally, benefits to selected interests were great. High tariffs assured a supply monopoly to the great chemical combines like Montecatini and to producers of agricultural machinery like Fiat.

Social and Economic Conditions, 1926–29

There can be little doubt that the policies of the regime adversely affected the great mass of Italian peasants and workers. These policies worked to isolate industrial workers, to divide the peasantry, and to cultivate the middle and lower bourgeoisie. Employers used the control over the work force granted them by Fascist terror tactics to introduce into their plants labor-efficiency methods imported from America. Unlike the American New Deal, however, Italian fascism did not have to respond to an independent labor constituency. It rejected the option of developing internal consumption by wage incentives. Instead, Italian industry used the autonomy it had obtained to parcel out the internal market by means of cartels. This strategy of development precluded Italy's entry into an era of mass production and consumption.

There was a decline in living standards for most workers. Beginning in 1927 with the quota 90, wage cuts were imposed regularly: 10 to 20 percent in October 1927, 8 percent in December 1930, and 7 percent in May 1934. Wholesale prices also declined between 1926 and 1928, which might have led to an increase in real wages had it not been for rising unemployment, shortened hours, and cuts in hourly pay coupled with widespread reclassification of workers into lower pay categories. Conditions for peasants were even worse. The result was a steady decline in the consumption of meat, fruit, vegetables, butter, sugar, wine, and coffee.[1]

Internal Migration

Despite the fact that the Fascists placed a high priority on social stability, the combination of low wages and stagnation in rural Italy forced vast internal migration. Italy under Mussolini proved to be as

---

1. On estimates of consumption, see Ester Fano Damascelli, "La restaurazione antifascista liberista," *Movimento di liberazione in Italia* 23 (1971): 52; Jon S. Cohen, "Fascism and Agriculture in Italy: Policies and Consequences," *Economic History Review* 32 (February 1979): 85; Cesare Vannutelli, "The Living Standard of Italian Workers," in *The Ax Within: Italian Fascism in Action*, ed. Roland Sarti (New York: New Viewpoints, 1974), pp. 156–57.

geographically mobile as other European countries. What made it unique was the Fascists' conscious effort to halt the process. Migration in Italy was a fact of life well before the coming of fascism, although it shifted from emigration abroad before World War I to internal migration after 1918. Between 1870 and 1911, Italy lost 35 percent of its natural population increase to emigration; by contrast, between 1931 and 1936, it lost only 15 percent. The closing of extra-European areas for emigration left few outlets for Italian migrants, but the flow continued within the country. There were about 600,000 changes of residence in 1923, 800,000 in 1926, 1 million between 1927 and 1929, and over 1 million annually during the troubled thirties.[2]

To curb this phenomenon the government gave powers to the prefects in 1928 to return those without means of support to their place of origin. In 1931 instructions went out to the prefects of Rome and Milan to apply all regulations limiting legal changes of residence. The combined opposition of industry, which disliked limitations on labor mobility, and of the Italians themselves, who were determined to escape rural stagnation, thwarted the regime. As a result, continued urban growth under fascism created widespread building speculation. Between 1921 and 1941, the population of Rome doubled. Massive reconstruction of the historic center of the city forced the poor into the periphery, where they merged with the new arrivals to form the famous Roman *borgate* (suburban slums). Milan and Turin experienced similar developments.

The Creation of a Fascist Union Organization

One of the great defects of the prefascist political ruling class was its lack of control over the labor force. Only the violence of the blackshirt squads broke the power of the Socialists and their General Confederation of Labor and restored the principle of social hierarchy to farm and factory. But this was largely a negative achievement, and in the large northern cities the hold of the regime over the working class was weak. It was not until 1926 that the last vestiges of democratic unionism were

2. Anna Treves, *Le migrazioni interne nell'Italia fascista* (Turin: Einaudi, 1976), pp. 17–19, 112–13.

eliminated. An alternative, Fascist-controlled union structure emerged in the cities relatively slowly (in contrast to rural areas). In 1919 and 1920 the Fascists occasionally supported the Unione Italiana del Lavoro, led by the syndicalist Alceste De Ambris, and the long-shoremen's union of Captain Giulietti. In 1921, when the Unione Italiana del Lavoro rejected fascism, one of its leaders, Edmondo Rossoni, broke away. A former syndicalist who had been active before World War I in the American Industrial Workers of the World (IWW), Rossoni, like Mussolini, converted to the myth of the revolutionary war during 1915. In January 1922, he emerged as head of a newly formed Confederazione dei Sindacati Nazionali, which included five national corporations for industry, agriculture, commerce, intellectuals and professionals, and longshoremen. Shortly before the March on Rome, the Fascist unions had roughly 500,000 members, but half were from agriculture and included landowners, tenants, and day laborers. (The Socialist leagues had been reduced to 300,000 members.) The bulk of organized nonagricultural labor continued to be enrolled in the Socialist unions, even though the CGL had declined from over 2 million members in 1920 to 400,000 in 1922.

Throughout 1923 and 1924 Mussolini still wanted to incorporate the CGL into his majority. Only after the Matteotti murder destroyed any chance of accommodation with the Socialist union leaders did the Fascist syndicalists have their first great opportunity. As we have seen, the attitude of the industrialists toward the growth of the Fascist unions was lukewarm at best. In 1923, Rossoni launched his drive to create syndical structures that would have included both workers and employers (integral syndicates), but the Confindustria acted to force the abandonment of the idea through the Palazzo Chigi Accords of December 1923. During the Matteotti crisis of 1924, Rossoni again harassed the employers with a number of strikes, until the industrialists and Mussolini came to terms in mid-1925. Eventually, however, the collapse of the Socialist General Confederation of Labor, which had been reduced to 200,000 members by 1925, opened the way to a monopoly for the Fascist unions formalized by the Vidoni Accord of October 2, 1925.

One major step remained to be taken. Justice Minister Rocco had argued as early as 1914 that the state could never be secure until it controlled the vast power of worker organizations and subjected the intermediate elite groups within the union bureaucracy to state direction. Only by making these unions into legally recognized and regulated entities would the state ensure that no external force would intervene, as the Socialists had done under the liberal system. Therefore Rocco denied any independent role to the Fascist unions in the syndical legislation of April 3, 1926, which made the unions legal agents of the state, established a compulsory system of arbitration, and banned strikes and lockouts. The legislation also set up a system of labor courts to resolve conflicts that could not be solved by negotiation or conciliation. The Rocco law extended official recognition to only one organization of workers and employers in each category of production. Almost by indirection, the Fascist government created an outline of a corporative system, but without creating a formal system of corporations. What existed in 1926 was a framework for labor relations. To oversee this first step, the government created, on July 2, 1926, a Ministry of Corporations.

The Emergence of the Corporative System and the Charter of Labor, 1926-29

Under the Rocco law the Confederation of Italian Industry was also allowed to consolidate its position as the dominant force in the private economic sphere. Small producers and craftsmen employing more than five workers were included in the Confindustria for purposes of representation. Moreover, this vast expansion of the Confindustria's power took place without any counterbalancing control by the Fascists over its internal organization.

A far different fate awaited Rossoni's syndical confederation. By 1927 the 2.4-million-member labor organization was the largest mass movement in Italy. Its size was equaled only by Rossoni's ambitions, as he strove to make the unions, rather than the party, the link between the masses and the state. By reaching for the post of minister of corporations, Rossoni attempted to control the entire system of labor-management relations. If he had been allowed to move unchecked, there would have been a serious crisis between the government and the industrialists. In an effort to thwart Rossoni, the Duce named himself as minister of corporations in 1926 and appointed Giuseppe Bottai as his undersecretary later that same year. Bottai, one of the most able of the Fascist leaders, was an opponent of Rossoni. He believed that the motor of the corporative system should be in a bureaucracy of managers and technocrats, who would work with their counterparts in industry and labor to direct the economy. This managerial theory of Fascist corporativism was perfectly compatible with private enterprise, but it demanded that the Ministry of Corporations gain a substantial degree of leverage over both labor and management.

In 1927 three conceptions of the role of the state in the economy clashed. On the one side were the Confindustria and Alfredo Rocco. In the middle was the corporative and technocratic position of Bottai. On the left were the syndicalists. The first test of strength between these positions came in early 1927 over the drafting of the *Carta del Lavoro*, the Labor Charter. This document, which was designed as a sort of "bill of rights" for labor, was intended to counter the negative international and domestic consequences of revaluation, forced salary reductions, and the suppression of free unions. Bottai was given the task of drawing up the document, but he was unable to resolve the conflict between the positions of the industrialists, who opposed anything more than a platonic statement of intent, and that of the unions, which wanted a precise set of legally binding gains for labor. Rocco was finally assigned to work out the final document that met the demands of the industrial employers. The Charter of Labor set forth the principle that relations between labor and management were to be governed by collectve contracts worked out between legally recognized organizations. It reaffirmed the primacy of private initiative and allowed state intervention only where the private sector was inadequate. In a final section the charter listed several nonbinding goals to be included in future legislation or collective agreements, such as guaranteed weekly rest periods, limitations on night labor, annual paid vacations, and improvements in social insurance, but with no provision for immediate realization.

The Break-Up of the Fascist Unions, 1928

The balance of power reflected in both the Rocco law of 1926 and the

Labor Charter of 1927 was decidedly unfavorable to the Fascist syndical movement, although the destruction of the power base of the Fascist unions only became inevitable when the regime began to draft legislation to reform the Chamber of Deputies. The new electoral machinery provided for a list of candidates to be submitted by the various officially recognized economic associations and by other public-interest organizations. Out of a list of one thousand nominees, the Fascist Grand Council would choose the four hundred names to be submitted to the voters on a take-it-or-leave-it basis. Under these provisions, Rossoni's labor organization, as the single largest economic association, would control an enormous number of nominations. In November 1928, the government decided to break the large confederation into six smaller federations for industry, agriculture, commerce, land transport and internal navigation, banking, and sea and air transport. Most of the old syndicalist leadership around Rossoni lost power, and the political weight of the unions was almost completely destroyed.

The consequences of this move against the unions were great. From an organization of almost three million, led by a politically ambitious Rossoni, the unions were reduced to an impotent series of small federations. The future development of the corporative system was also compromised because any countervailing power to that of the employers was lost. The Fascist corporativists, who envisaged for themselves a role as mediator between capital and labor, were henceforth confronted by unchecked management power that was totally opposed to an expansion of the corporative system. The workers, unable to elect their own leaders, and alienated by wage reductions, lost faith in the unions, which became a form of employment for lower-middle-class bureaucrats.

The Domestication of the Fascist Party, 1925–30

If the result of Fascist policy between 1926 and 1929 was the creation of a series of limited, semiautonomous power centers under the mediation of Mussolini, it was necessary to integrate the Fascist party into this overall pattern. Mussolini had a relatively easy time controlling the central organization of the party, but he found it harder to rein in the ras and their squads. His control was gradually extended between 1922 and 1930 until the party was totally domesticated.

In the first period, from October 1922 until June 1924, Mussolini used the squads in order to intimidate any opposition, but his major aim during this period seems to have been the stabilization of Fascist power. The reorganization of the party's central apparatus by the creation of the Fascist Grand Council and the establishment of a secretariat directly answerable to Mussolini were efforts to assure control over the PNF. For most of this early period, Mussolini tried various combinations of collective leadership with no single party secretary. Under the circumstances, Mussolini could move against the power of the ras sporadically because of his continuing need for the squads as a weapon against opposition. Only when provincial leaders, like Padovani in Naples, threatened to upset relations with the conservatives, or when Gino Baroncini in Bologna had powerful rivals within his own organization, could Mussolini move against a local leader.

The Matteotti murder altered the situation drastically. Mussolini's own secretariat was tainted by scandal, and the intransigents, led by Roberto Farinacci, emerged as the dominant faction at the party conference in August 1924. The culmination of the intransigents' victory came with the appointment of Farinacci as party secretary on February 12, 1925. Farinacci, a former railroad worker and exsocialist, was head of the Fascist movement in Cremona. Unlike Dino Grandi, Giuseppe Bottai, or Italo Balbo, Farinacci never adjusted to the social and political compromises with the traditional order. He had his brief moment as secretary of the party, but his violent and erratic personality precluded nomination to national office. Farinacci obtained his law degree by copying another student's thesis, and, during the Ethiopian war, he managed to lose a hand while fishing with grenades. (Of course, he was decorated for injuries incurred in action.) In 1925 his appointment seemed to signify that the lower-middle-class provincial fascists were about to come into their own on the national scene. A dangerous rivalry might have developed between Luigi Federzoni, the conservative interior minister, and Farinacci for control of the mechanism of repression, but Mussolini made it clear that he would support state over party power.

Under Farinacci, centralization of party control in the secretariat was completed. At the fourth and final congress of the PNF, on June 21–22, 1925, all decisions were made unanimously with little discussion. Farinacci's authoritarian disposition also discouraged debate on any level of the party. Henceforth offices were filled by appointment from above rather than by election.

A clash between Mussolini's conception of a party totally subservient to the state and Farinacci's ambition to have the party take over the state was bound to come. Two issues arose to crystallize their differences. One of Farinacci's first moves as secretary in 1925 was to close membership rolls at a particularly delicate moment when many conservatives desired to join the winning side. Farinacci expressed the fears of the old guard that the party would be swamped in the tide of new recruits. In 1925 party membership declined from 650,000 to 600,000, but the ban was lifted by Mussolini on March 30, 1926, the day on which Farinacci resigned as secretary. Membership then grew rapidly in 1926 and 1927 to reach one million.

The second issue that revealed a conflict between Mussolini and his party secretary arose over Farinacci's toleration of violent repression outside of the official mechanism of the Interior Ministry. On October 3–5, 1925, in front of horrified foreign tourists, the Florentine squads went on a rampage against the opposition, leaving several dead and many injured. Mussolini, who was trying to cultivate his image abroad, ordered a demobilization of the squads and the removal of the local party leader. By the end of the year, Mussolini searched only for a pretext to dump Farinacci as well. It came when the secretary led the defense team of Amerigo Dumini, Matteotti's murderer. The trial ended on March 24, 1926. A week later Farinacci, who understood that his days were numbered, resigned. The departure of a man whom Mussolini detested pointed up a curious feature of the regime and of Mussolini's personality. The Duce was incapable of physically exterminating his opponents within the party, as Hitler exterminated Ernst Röhm and the chiefs of the SA in the "Blood Purge" of June 1934. Farinacci left somewhat bruised, but alive and unbroken. From his base in Cremona he continued to offer Mussolini unwanted advice on policy.

The Turati Era, 1926–30

Farinacci's successor as party secretary was Augusto Turati, the party leader in Brescia, who had ties to the labor movement. In 1926 Turati had several virtues and few vices from Mussolini's point of view. He was an enemy of the union chief Rossoni and of Farinacci, but was not a dominant figure in the PNF. He also did not make the mistake of considering himself practically Mussolini's equal as had Farinacci. Moreover, Turati was an efficient administrator who could be counted on to make the centralized machinery run well. Under Turati the remaining provincial power centers were liquidated. The formal role of the PNF increased, while its real political power atrophied. The new statute, which the PNF received in October 1926, ratified the changes. Mussolini became absolute head of the movement, and the Grand Council, by now reduced to rubber-stamp status, kept formal power to make policy. Appointment to all offices came from higher levels. Severe limitations were put on the powers of the provincial leaders (*federali*) and on the local fasci to act independently. Mussolini made painfully clear the limited role he intended for the PNF on January 5, 1927, in a circular to the prefects in which he referred to them as "the highest authority of the state in the province" and to the party as an instrument of state policy.

A major step in the incorporation of the party into the state apparatus came with the Law on the Powers of the Grand Council of December 9, 1928, which turned the party governing body into a state organ, presided over by the Head of Government. The Grand Council would choose the four hundred members of the Chamber of Deputies, nominate the party secretary and other high officials of the PNF, participate in decisions over changes in the succession to the throne, in the powers of the king, the head of government, the Grand Council itself, and the houses of parliament. Finally, it had the right to present to the Crown a list of nominees for the post of Head of Government. The scope of this law might have indicated a takeover of the state by the party. Actually, it meant that the independent role of the Grand Council and of the PNF was exhausted. The Council met more infrequently after 1929 and was never allowed to draw up a list of possible successors to Mussolini, although Farinacci, to Mussolini's annoyance, occasionally raised the subject. Only once, on July 25, 1943, did it become a truly deliberative body and then it was to write the last act of the Fascist regime by voting against Mussolini and opening the way for the king to name Marshall Badoglio as successor.

An area of potentially great power for the party involved efforts to compete with the labor unions in organizing workers. In April 1927, the PNF took over supervision of the Opera Nazionale Dopolavoro (OND), the leisure-time and social organization of the masses. The effort met with some success, as Victoria De Grazia's recent work on the Dopolavoro reveals. The organization was divided into industrial and white-collar sections. Because the industrial branch was controlled within the plants by the employers, the OND was favored by industry over unions as a safe outlet for worker activity. Here again, however, formal supervision of the Dopolavoro only masked the reality of its being a management-controlled organization designed to divide the workers and weaken the attraction of unions.

Finally, the party assumed a major role in physical education and sport when it became involved in 1926 with the Opera Nazionale Balilla, an organization for young people from six to eighteen years of age. In 1930 the PNF extended its mission with the creation of the Fascio Giovanile di Combattimento for the eighteen to twenty-one age group, but in the meantime it lost control of the Balilla, which became a semiautonomous part of the Ministry of National Education from 1929 to 1937.

Turati's term as secretary of the PNF ended on October 8, 1930, when he was replaced by Giovanni Giuriati. During this period Mussolini succeeded in creating a party that was almost completely devoid of political initiative. The chronic rebelliousness that had been characteristic of the party as late as 1925 was a thing of the past. Yet, despite its improved administrative structure, the party did not serve as an effective link between the government and the masses or as a true training ground for the Fascist political elite.

Conciliation: The Vatican State within the State, 1929

The final step toward a stable relationship with the major social and economic institutions came with the Lateran accords of February 1929, between the Vatican and the Italian government. Efforts to reach an understanding, which had resumed after the Matteotti crisis, were facilitated by the elimination of the Italian Popular party. A formal solution to the Pope's status in Rome and to Church-state relations in general appealed to both sides. The Fascist regime achieved three objectives by concluding its bargain with the Catholic Church. First, it was able to incorporate the last major center of considerable independent power within the framework of the regime. Second, the regime was able to use the Church's links to the rural masses and to the middle class to reinforce its own hold over the population. Finally, the Fascist state increased its international prestige. The Vatican also made several short- and long-term gains. It settled the Roman question and obtained the creation of the Vatican state, as well as a number of specific guarantees for the rights of Catholic schools, the central position of the Catholic religion in the teaching curriculum of the elementary and middle schools, and inclusion of church law in Italian legislation on divorce. By winning recognition for its semiautonomous sphere, the Church built its own subculture through institutions like the Catholic University of Milan, the Catholic Action organization, the Federation of Catholic University Students, and through a growing number of journals and periodicals. In short, it created under fascism the nucleus of what would become the post–World War II political class.

Negotiations for the Lateran Treaty and the Concordat began in mid-1926 and were concluded in February 1929. Settlements on major points came with relative ease, except for the problem of Catholic youth organizations. In this case the Church reluctantly conceded that all sporting and physical education activities would be reserved to the Balilla. The Lateran Treaty laid the basis for a friendly relationship between state and Church until 1943. That is not to say that no disagreements arose. In 1931 a major dispute developed over the youth sections of Catholic Action, which the Church had not brought completely into line with the Lateran accords. A second crisis developed over the racial legislation of 1938, which the papacy condemned and the Catholic Church worked silently to sabotage. But the Church hierarchy supported the upsurge of nationalism during the Ethiopian war and responded favorably to Italian intervention against the

Spanish Republic in 1936. On balance, the Catholic Church was a valuable ally of the regime.

The Plebiscite of 1929

On March 24, 1929, elections for a new Chamber of Deputies were held. The list of candidates presented to the voters had been selected by the Grand Council from the nominations made by the various syndical, professional, and political organizations. The final list of four hundred names provided an indication of the winners and losers in the consolidation of the Fascist regime. Geographically, the North with 178 deputies outdistanced the South and the islands (119) and the Center (50), but the city of Rome alone, with its swollen bureaucracy, had 50 deputies. The subordinate position of the working class was revealed in the new parliament: landowners received 46 seats to the farm laborers' 27; industrialists had 31, while the workers received 26. Similar numerical advantages were given to employers in commerce, banking, and services. Even more striking was the effort to reward the professional middle class and the veterans. The Confederation of Professions and Artists was assigned 82 seats and the major veterans' associations 40. There was, however, no vast turnover in the political class. Although only 196 members of the old chamber were returned, 50 others were named to the senate, 14 entered the diplomatic corps, 5 became prefects, and only 60 were dropped entirely.[3]

3. Renzo De Felice, *Mussolini il fascista*, vol. 2, *L'organizzazione dello stato fascista* (Turin: Einaudi, 1968), pp. 476–77.

Chapter Five
*The Fascist Regime
and the
Great Depression
1929–34*

As the dictatorship was being consolidated, Mussolini dealt separately with a range of private interests. Each was integrated into the regime through the creation of areas of semiautonomy. Mussolini became mediator between social and economic elite groups. Prominent members of the Fascist party were rewarded by high office, but they most often identified with the state rather than with the party. The PNF itself lost most of its political initiative and was relegated to routine administrative tasks. This system of government, created between 1925 and 1929, tended to increase the power of the state over public life through the monopoly of the Fascist party, the establishment of press censorship, and control over labor organizations. In contrast, the state continued to respect the bastions of conservative power (monarchy, army, private industrial holdings) and even retreated from the claims of the liberal state in order to reach accord with the Catholic Church.

The Fascists were wont to call their new order "totalitarian," but this term needs to be understood in context. In theory, the Fascists meant that all political, social, and economic relations were carried on through institutions established or controlled by the regime. In practice, for most of conservative Italy the totalitarian dimension meant tacking the title "fascist" onto preexisting organizations. Only the industrial working class and the northern radicalized peasantry felt the full weight of the dictatorship. But the onset of the depression and the rapid deterioration of the Versailles system altered the carefully worked-out compromises of the 1920s concerning the relationship of public to private power and changed fascism's own self image of its exclusively national mission.

Fascism Comes of Age:
"The Ministry of All the Talents," March 1929

In March 1929, as if to symbolize the regime's new-found stability, Mussolini orchestrated a vast governmental reorganization in which he gave up seven of the eight ministries under his control and promoted his undersecretaries to ministerial rank: Dino Grandi to Foreign Affairs, Giuseppe Bottai to Corporations, Michele Bianchi to Public Works, Italo Balbo to Aviation, Costanzo Ciano to Communications, Antonio Mosconi to Finance. Alfredo Rocco continued as minister of justice and Mussolini as Head of Government and interior minister. The new government was exceptionally young (Bottai, Balbo, and Grandi were in their early thirties). As if to emphasize its claim as the first truly "fascist" ministry, three leaders of the March on Rome (Balbo, De Bono, and Bianchi) were included. Finally, the participation of Rocco, Bottai, Grandi, and Balbo gave the new government a particularly activist stamp, and brought together the best talents of the regime as well.

The promotion of Bottai reflected this resolve to accentuate the Fascist character of policy. The Ministry of Corporations was the unique creation of the regime. On its success rode any hope of major economic and social innovation under fascism. Bottai, a man of vast ambition, now had the difficult task of reconciling the aspirations of the Fascist managers with the iron resolve of the industrialists to defend their autonomy. For a moment it seemed that the world depression of 1929 would provide an opening for corporative experimentation.

The Corporative Illusion, 1929–34

Corporativism can be defined as a system of institutional arrangements by which capital and labor are integrated into obligatory, hierarchical, and functional units (corporations), recognized by the state, which become organs of self-government for issues relating to the specific grouping as well as the basis for participation with other corporatively organized interests in policy decisions affecting the whole society (corporative parliament). The corporations may be the controlling element in the state or they may be, as in Italy, controlled by a political authority which exists independently of and outside the corporative system.

The only serious attempt to realize a corporative policy in Italy occurred between 1929 and 1932 under Giuseppe Bottai. By 1934 it became evident that the corporative system had fallen far short of its objectives. At the end of 1929, the Ministry of Corporations supervised associations that had a combined membership of over four million, but the system itself was still in its initial stages. The beginning of the corporative order was the reform of the National Council of Corporations (CNC) in March 1930. The CNC was to become a sort of corporative parliament. It was organized as a three-tiered system: at the base were seven sections that were the existing employer and worker organizations in each branch of the economy; a second level comprised a general assembly made up of representatives of economic associations, of social and welfare institutions, of the PNF, and of the state bureaucracy; at the top was the Central Corporative Committee under Mussolini's direction and composed of government ministers, the presidents of the various confederations of workers and employers, career civil servants, and officials of the PNF. The structure was relatively simple in so far as it used the existing economic associations as the basic units and sought only to integrate them at higher levels.

Bottai wanted the state to determine policy and to set the parameters within which the workers and employers would act. But labor emerged from the struggles of the twenties so weakened and management so strong that the corporative machinery had little leverage over the employers unless Mussolini intervened. Faced with the prospect of a confrontation with the industrialists, Mussolini refused to allow the corporative institutions to determine policy. At that point the very simplicity of the structure became an acute embarrassment that could only be disguised by making it more complex. This was accomplished in the reform of February 5, 1934, which established twenty-two corporations, each acting as a small parliament with nominal power over wages and conditions of labor within the productive category and serving as a vehicle for conciliation between divergent interests. The corporations were divided into three large sections to correspond with agriculture, industry, and services. However, only the employer associations really defended the interests of their members, and they preferred to deal with important issues outside of the corporative system. The labor unions with their appointed officials fought only rearguard actions.

Corporativism and the Great Depression: The "Third Way"

Fascist propagandists constantly referred to corporativism as a "third way" between communism and capitalism. "Rome or Moscow," fascism or bolshevism, were the "revolutionary" alternatives for a decaying, liberal Europe. Yet, when it came to dealing with the effects of the depression, the corporative system proved totally irrevelant.

Italy had only just recovered from the effects of rigidly deflationary policies, which had curbed the boom of the mid-twenties, when the economic crisis hit. As a result, its impact was somewhat muted but nonetheless severe. Between 1929 and 1933 stock prices lost 39 percent of their value (less than in other countries where the base was higher). The index of manufacturing production (1938=100) stood at 90 in 1929, but fell to 77 in 1931 and 1932, and rose only slightly in 1933 to 82. Italian foreign trade also suffered. Imports were off 29 percent and exports down one quarter, but comparable figures for exports showed Germany down 49 percent, France 51 percent, the United States 64 percent, and Japan 53 percent. Because Italy imported mainly raw materials, which fell in price more rapidly than industrial goods, exports covered 80 percent of Italian imports in 1932 against only 70 percent in 1929, but the heavy dependency on these same imported raw materials made it difficult to ease the chronic trade deficit. To make matters worse, monetary transfers from Italians abroad dried up. Reserves of the Bank of Italy dropped by one third. The budget, which had been balanced in 1929, underwent a transformation as government spending increased rapidly and unemployment rose from 300,000 in 1929 to one million in 1933. Expenditures for public works rose from one eighth to one quarter of total spending, while the military budget dropped from 31 to 25 percent.

The improvised responses of the Fascist regime to the depression resembled those of other industrial nations and built on past policies. To some extent, the uniquely "fascist" quality of the economic remedies can be seen in the degree of intensity with which certain policies were pushed and in the freedom from popular pressure that an authoritarian regime enjoyed. Thus, as elsewhere, there was a marked tendency toward further state intervention in the economy. Fascism's preference for heavy industry and the historic reliance of that sector on state aid in the form of tariff protection and subsidies made direct government intervention natural, but the extent of public ownership was unprecedented. Next, fascism encouraged the concentration and rationalization of the private industrial sectors by means of state-sponsored cartels. The government also resorted to tariff protection and currency controls. Finally, wages were kept low and consumption was sacrificed to the needs of heavy industry.

Italian economic policy differed from that of the American New Deal to the extent that Roosevelt's large popular base in the labor movement led him to concentrate on projects that would have an immediate impact on incomes and consumption. Public ownership was kept to a minimum, and semicorporative attempts at industrial regulation, such as the NRA, were declared unconstitutional. Nazi policy more closely resembled that of Italian fascism in the encouragement given to cartelization and planning, but again there was less state ownership.

State Intervention in Italy:
The Istituto per la Ricostruzione Industriale

Massive state intervention with little regard for the corporative system was the most notable feature of Fascist policy during the depression. The reasons for this are tied to the historically close connection that had developed between heavy industry and a few large banks, like the Banca Commerciale, the Banca Italiana di Sconto, and the Credito Italiano. These banks held large, often controlling, blocks of stock in many of the great corporations and therefore were susceptible to industrial crisis. The collapse of Ansaldo, a giant holding company in steel and engineering, brought down the Banca Italiana di Sconto in

1921. By the mid-twenties, special institutions to bail out the banks operated with limited funds. However, the onset of the depression and the collapse of stock values put enormous pressure on the banks, which then tried to enter the market to sustain industrial values. These efforts only made the problem worse by decreasing the liquidity of the major financial institutions. Prolonged depression revealed the fatal flaw in the entire system of industrial financing that tied up bank capital in long-term industrial activities. The severe strain on the banks threatened all private investors and savers. By the end of 1931 the situation was critical. On December 4, 1931, the state stepped in by forming the Istituto Mobiliare Italiano (IMI), which was empowered to absorb some of the industrial paper held by the banks. Unfortunately, even with a large starting capital, the IMI could not stop the hemorrhaging. The two largest banks, the Banca Commerciale and the Credito Italiano, had exhausted their resources, and the IMI could no longer help.

On January 23, 1933, the Fascist regime took what turned out to be a decisive step in the relationship between the state and the private economy when it set up the Istituto per la Ricostruzione Industriale (IRI). The IRI took over the large stock holdings of the banks, as well as companies on the verge of bankruptcy. Under this curious system the state became a stockholder along with private capital, but very often its single bloc of stock gave it controlling interest. By 1939, 70 percent of pig iron production, 45 percent of steel, 80 percent of naval construction, almost all shipping, and parts of the electrical and telephone industries were in the hands of the state. Only extremely profitable sectors were eventually turned back to private capital.

Obviously, such an invasion by the state, albeit involuntary and necessary, aroused great fears among the industrialists and high expectations among supporters of the corporative system. Mussolini clarified his intentions when he appointed Alberto Beneduce as IRI's first director. Beneduce was a former Social Democrat, a member of Bonomi's 1921 cabinet, and an antifascist until after the Matteotti crisis. He was also president of a large electrical company in southern Italy and had little interest in the corporative system. In short, he was ideal for the mission of reorganizing and managing the huge state holdings without threatening private enterprise.

Cartelization

Despite the creation of the IRI, the regime respected its basic arrangements with heavy industry, but it began to integrate industries into a political system over which the industrialists had only limited control. With state permission, almost every sector of industry and agriculture was organized into production and marketing cartels. Growers of hemp, rice, sugar beets, and silk formed producer cartels, but it was in industry that the major concentrations took place (steel, cement, marble, rayon, shipping).

The state's role in this process was important. Under a law of June 16, 1932, firms that controlled 70 percent of production in a given branch of industry or agriculture could ask for state intervention to make cartel agreements obligatory for all other firms in the same field. On January 12, 1933, the government required firms that planned expansion of facilities or construction of new plants to obtain prior consent. This theoretical extension of governmental power was, in reality, a way of closing out firms from entering markets and upsetting cartel agreements. Since many of the industrial sectors were already controlled by one or two firms—Montecatini in chemicals and pharmaceuticals, Pirelli in rubber, Snia Viscosa and Montecatini in synthetics, Fiat in autos—the combination of private and state action only ratified the existing concentrations of private power and destroyed incentives for innovation by maintaining high prices and market shares. Eventually, in 1936, the state demanded that cartels which controlled 75 percent of production or more report to the corporations about their activities, but because the corporative system was either inoperative or in the hands of the cartels, the provision remained a dead letter.

Restraints on Trade

The universal economic remedy during the depression was to resort to tariffs and other restraints on trade. The United States, France, and Great Britain all raised tariffs in 1931 and 1932. Italian dependence on imported raw materials and the consequent vulnerability of her industrial base led the Fascists to move even more emphatically in this direction. Italy's problems, however, were not entirely caused by factors beyond the control of the government. For political reasons the Fascist regime refused to abandon the gold standard or its support for the overvalued lira. The refusal to devalue was an additional burden and forced the government to seek other means to deal with the negative balance-of-payments situation. Four methods were used: dumping (selling abroad at prices well below the domestic market price), increased tariffs, exchange controls, and an active effort to expand markets in central and eastern Europe to make up for lost trade in the West.

The Standard of Living

The disruption brought to the economy by the depression meant that the Fascist state was forced into a more active role in controlling the labor force. Official policy called for reductions in wages and prices, but for the average worker, retail prices did not move downward as rapidly as prices on the wholesale level. Reduced hours of work meant smaller paychecks. Reports of additional unofficial wage reductions imposed by employers were common in the Fascist labor press. The government sought to compensate workers by expanding leisure time activities and family allowances. Appeals to the masses through the controlled media, as well as police surveillance, were intensified.

As unemployment rose from 300,000 in 1929 to over a million in 1933, the regime struggled to find a solution to the crisis that would not threaten the state's basic economic policies. Because Italy had a notoriously high percentage of underemployed, especially in agriculture, there was little likelihood of shifting workers back to the farms. Nor would emigration offer any respite. Between 1931 and 1936, emigration took much less of the natural increase in population than in earlier years. The nature of Fascist industrial growth made it difficult for heavy industry to absorb workers at a faster rate. Only the service sector offered a solution which, coupled with the expanded economic role of the state, helps explain why fascism took on increasingly bureaucratic features.

Peasants

Most severely hit by the depression were the agricultural workers, who faced wage reductions of from 20 to 40 percent. Not unexpectedly, the crisis had a dampening effect on the ruralization program. Rural unemployment, always staggeringly high outside of the harvest and planting seasons, drove peasants into the cities. The regime attempted to counter this exodus by encouraging more peasants to become tenant farmers. Plots of reclaimed land were distributed to families of landless laborers, but little could be done to raise standards under the deteriorating conditions of the agricultural market. Major efforts were made to enroll women in Fascist peasant organizations on the theory that they might act as stabilizing elements within the family. But, even here, ugly relaities intruded on the idyllic picture which fascism tried to paint of the peasant woman. Wages for female agricultural workers were about one half those of male workers. One of the rare, partially successful strikes during the depression period was waged in 1931 by female rice harvesters (*mondine*) in the Po Valley, who rebelled against cuts in their subsistence wages.

As a means of dealing with the rural problem, the government allowed the PNF to control rural schools in order to propagate the advantages of social stability. The PNF also created the Commissariato per le Migrazioni e la Colonizzazione Interna in April 1931 to channel individuals and families from provinces with excess population into areas of land reclamation or into the South and the islands, but lack of development in these areas offered little hope of a permanent solution. The Fascists fell back on a series of merely repressive measures which ineffectually sought to keep people in place. For instance, in 1935 a workbook (*libretto di lavoro*) was introduced to curb labor mobility. Laws were passed to make it almost impossible to officially move into a town of more than twenty-five thousand inhabitants or into an industrial center. In order to reside in a city, one had to have already secured a position, but in order to gain employment, a person had to have a residence in the city. Nevertheless, into this "catch 22" world slipped millions of Italians who populated the slums around Rome, Milan, and Turin.

Industrial Workers and White-Collar Employees

Industrial workers fared better than peasants, but conditions of labor and diet declined for them as well. High unemployment, sweatshop conditions in small artisan production, and the weakness of labor organization gave employers almost absolute power over the work force. In large-scale industry, this freedom was used to introduce new efficiency and timesaving methods, like the Bedeaux system of timed piecework, which was imposed over the bitter "objections of the Fascist unions because it increased stress on the job. Repression of the working class might have been greater had not the state, the PNF, and private industry often worked at cross purposes. Employers successfully fought to keep the workers divided and the PNF and the Fascist unions in a subordinate position. Only in 1939 were union shop representatives (*fiduciari di fabbrica*) officially readmitted within the plants in a partial reversal of the Vidoni Accord of 1925.

Salaries for managers, technical workers, and state bureaucrats tended to be reduced less severely than blue-collar wages. There was also constant expansion in the number of state employees as well as those in parastate agencies, the PNF, and the syndicates. Large numbers of lower-middle-class workers entered a system that placed primary stress on hierarchy and political loyalty. In return, compensation came in the form of relatively higher wages and fringe benefits.

Conclusion on the Economy during the Depression

The Fascist regime altered the role of the state in Italian economic life. These changes were largely forced on the regime by events, such as the collapse of the banking system, rather than implemented by any preconceived plan. When the state took control of a large part of the industrial base, it attempted to respect the rules of the capitalist economy. In the long run, however, the regime gained control of powerful instruments—control of credit and the operation of the IRI—which it later used to direct the economy according to foreign policy aims quite distinct from those of the industrialists. Yet, even within that new framework, the privileged economic sectors, which had emerged in the 1920s, continued to dominate. Fascism created a complex system in which the public and private bureaucracies interacted behind a facade of corporative organization.

The Changing Role of the Fascist Party

Between the end of 1929 and 1934 there were three secretaries of the PNF: Augusto Turati, who left office in October 1930; Giovanni Giuriati, who headed the party until December 7, 1931; and Achille Starace, who remained secretary until the end of October 1939. Each man moved the party further into the bureaucratic structure of the state. Under Turati the power of the local ras was definitively broken, but Turati's conception of the party as an active force within the unions and the corporations was far too ambitious for Mussolini's taste. The Duce never allowed the creation of an independent power center in the Fascist party, nor did he allow party radicals to disrupt the basic compromises with the industrialists or the Catholic Church.

Turati's successor, Giuriati, was a former Nationalist, who had been second in command to D'Annunzio at Fiume in 1919. Although he had served in several cabinet-level positions under Mussolini, he lacked the authority of Farinacci or Turati. Inevitably, under Giuriati, the party lost ground in policy making, although it continued to expand its bureaucracy by building up student and women's organizations. However, Giuriati too ran afoul of Mussolini during the dispute with the Vatican in 1931 over Catholic youth organizations. Finally, with the emergence of Achille Starace, the Duce found the perfect match of man with moment. Starace had been a party official since the early 1920s, but only in a political movement devoid of any policy initiative could he emerge as leader. A toady in his relationship with Mussolini, mean and authoritarian toward others, universally despised, Starace was bombastic, a lover of boots and uniforms, of parades and mass demonstrations (but with none of Goebbels's genius). In short, he was Mussolini's perfect choice to head a PNF that mobilized only for carefully orchestrated events. After 1932, membership in the party became ever more a matter of opportunism, or a sine qua non for a job. The PNF's main duty was to perpetuate the myth of the Duce. For that purpose, unthinking, ritual behavior (Storace's strong suit) became the norm. The revised party statutes of 1932 reinforced the already centralized administration and the personal role of Mussolini, while devaluing previously important party organs, like the Grand Council.

Starace's notion of success was measured in numbers. By 1939 the youth groups under the umbrella organization, *Gioventù Italiana del Littorio*, had almost 8 million members, the university groups reached 100,000, the PNF 2,500,000, with an additional 750,000 in female sections and about 1,500,000 in the organization for peasant women, the *Massaie Rurali*. Membership in the *Opera Nazionale Dopolavoro* grew even more rapidly, from just under 300,000 in 1926 to 5,000,000 in 1940. It ran 1,227 theaters, 771 movie houses, 2,130 orchestras, 6,427 libraries, and 11,159 sporting groups. Nothing like it had ever existed in Italy, and, while the Dopolavoro did not create the kind of active commitment which might save the regime in a crisis, it represented an innovative social experiment.

The Limits of Fascist Consensus:
Mussolini and the Role of the Fascist Government

During the 1930s, as the middle echelon of the PNF was deprived of any creative function, a kind of paralysis, bred by cynicism, crept up through the official organs of the regime. Larger numbers of Italians understood that fascism lacked any real commitment to social and economic change. The period between 1929 and 1934 was pivotal in this regard. What began in 1929 as the most ambitious governmental reshaping in the history of the regime ended abruptly in July 1932 with the dismissal of the "ministry of all the talents." Grandi was replaced by Mussolini as foreign minister. Alfredo Rocco, responsible for much of the institutional framework of fascism, but old and ailing, handed the Justice Ministry to a jurist without political influence. Giuseppe Bottai, whose taste for corporativism far outstripped that of either Mussolini or the industrialists, was dismissed from his post as minister of corporations. In a partial reversion to earlier practice, Mussolini personally took over both Foreign Affairs and Corporations.

The Duce also became more isolated after the death of his brother Arnaldo in December 1931. As editor of the *Popolo d'Italia*, Arnaldo Mussolini had been the Duce's one trusted collaborator. Increasingly, those who had known Mussolini on a basis of equality were replaced by new men who knew him only as Duce. Such was the nature of the government. Power had been drained from the party into the traditional state apparatus. From there it had been concentrated in the hands of the justice and interior ministers and in the person of Mussolini. The crucial decisions made during the Matteotti crisis to come to terms with individual power centers rather than to challenge the old social and economic order meant that fascism increasingly took on the conservative function of mediating between established interests. The new political class and the Fascist party cadres found their roles circumscribed to mere administration of day-to-day affairs. For the functioning of such a system no meaningful innovations were needed or desired. In fact, it was risky even to define too precisely the central core of Fascist doctrine. Official pronouncements about fascism and corporativism could only be universally accepted once they had been drained of all content. Thus, only after Bottati's dissmissal as minister of corporations could the imposing, but meaningless, corporative reform of 1934 take place. In the end, all that could be passed down through the vast network of party, labor, and leisure-time organizations was the myth of the Duce. But this was too little for such an elaborate structure. The result was boredom and a sense of stagnation, which was acutely anticipated in 1929 by Alberto Moravia in his novel of aimless Roman youth, *Gli indifferenti (The Indifferent)*.

The Third Way and Universal Fascism

The depression years led to much speculation about the potential of corporativism as an alternative to both capitalism and communism. Perhaps the most interesting thinking about corporativism came out of journals like *Nuovi studi*, edited by Ugo Spirito and Arnaldo Volpicelli, Bottai's *Archivio di Studi Corporativi*, and various university-oriented publications, like *Il Cantiere*, *Il Saggiatore*, and *L'Universale*. Fascist reformers between 1930 and 1934 sought a sharper break with the past, more reliance on the post-1918 generation, and increased economic and social content for the Fascist revolution. More specifically, they urged that the weakness of the unions could only be overcome by restoring internal democracy. Another group of theorists around Spirito and Volpicelli concentrated on the corporations themselves. They called for corporative ownership of the means of production as a way of overcoming the concentration of private power and the split between the individual and society. Finally, all critics agreed that corporativism meant planning in a system that would reward technical and managerial ability with real power.

The onset of the depression and the crumbling liberal democratic order in Europe also led many Italians to see fascism as a sort of universal remedy. Among older Fascists this took the form of an effort to create a conservative front against bolshevism, but younger activists were attracted by the "revolutionary" mission of fascism in a decadent Europe. A movement for a Fascist International was pushed by organizations like the Action Committees for the Universality of Rome. The Fascists made an effort to bring together extreme right-wing movements in Europe under the leadership of Italy, but the Fascist International collapsed after a congress held in December 1934 at Montreux got totally out of control as disputes developed between conservative Catholics and racists. Thereafter the Italians lost ground in the fertile central European region to the more aggressive Nazis.

Chapter Six
*Fascist Foreign
Policy
1922–35*

When the Fascist movement took power in October 1922, little thought had been given to foreign policy. Hitler's years in the political wilderness before attaining power had allowed him ample time to brood over Germany's aims in central and eastern Europe, but Mussolini's activities before the March on Rome had brought him into only sporadic contact with foreign policy issues, and even this contact was that of an intelligent journalist whose primary concern was domestic policy.

As a result, Fascist foreign policy initially bore the imprint of professional diplomats, who were cautious about security problems in central Europe and who sought territorial concessions in the Middle East and Africa in cooperation with the Western Powers. The other major foreign policy influence on Italian fascism derived from the Italian Nationalist Association, which had supported imperialist expansion in Africa and in the Balkans even to the point of conflict with Great Britain and France. If the Foreign Office tended to moderate aggressive tendencies in fascism, the Nationalists worked against an understanding with Yugoslavia and toward revision of the Versailles Treaty. A third ingredient in Fascist foreign policy was Mussolini's own unstable personality; Mussolini viewed imperialism as a natural struggle among nations and saw the prestige of Italy in personal terms. He consciously used foreign policy as a means of stabilizing his hold over Italy by countering the activities of antifascist exiles and improving the image of the regime abroad.

The seizure of power by the Fascists in October 1922 marked no real break with the past. Until 1935 changes came gradually and affected style more than substance. As a relatively weak great power, Italy's position was traditionally enhanced when the European system was in rough equilibrium. However, throughout the 1920s this was not the case. France was the strongest continental power, and England dominated the Mediterranean Sea. A revival of German power could benefit Italy, but it raised a renewed threat to Austrian independence that Italy could not tolerate, for it would substitute for the relatively weak Austrian Republic one of Europe's great powers on the northeastern border. In such an international context, foreign policy gains could only be made directly through negotiations with the covictors of Versailles, or indirectly by playing England off against France, or by creating difficulties for France in eastern Europe that might force concessions elsewhere.

Relations with the Western Powers

Fascist foreign policy toward America was dictated by financial necessities arising out of the war debt owed by Italy and the need for American loans to aid the stabilization of the lira in 1925 and 1926. These twin aims were accomplished by an Italian mission to Washington in October 1925 that settled the debt question at a remarkably low interest rate and by a major loan from a banking consortium led by J. P. Morgan.

More central to Italian diplomacy were relations with England. With the collapse of Britain's pro-Greek policy in 1922, and after a conflict over the Italian seizure of the Greek island of Corfu in 1923, relations between Britain and Italy improved. Austen Chamberlain, an admirer of Mussolini, became British foreign secretary in 1924. With his help, several issues relating to war debts were ironed out, the British territory of Jubaland was transferred to Italian Somalia, and a slight rectification of the Egyptian-Libyan frontier was made. These crumbs were accepted by the Fascist regime in anticipation of British support for an eventual banquet in Ethiopia.

Far more troubled was Italy's relationship with France, which involved strategic interests in both the Mediterranean and in Danubian Europe. There was the festering sore of the large Italian community in

Tunisia, whose rights had been governed by an 1896 convention which France abrogated in 1918. France was also the preferred refuge for many of the antifascist exiles who, while not treated royally, were allowed a substantial amount of freedom in their political activities. But the core of the conflict was over central Europe. Mussolini resented Frence hegemony in the Danubian Basin and in the Balkans. For their part, the French were unwilling to make concessions in Africa to buy Italian support for their European alliance system. With neither side willing to yield, relations between France and Italy remained at an impasse until 1934, when German threats against Austria drew them together.

Italy, Yugoslavia, and the Little Entente

Nowhere did the contradictions among the various components of Fascist foreign policy emerge more glaringly than in relations with Yugoslavia. Initially, Mussolini broke with the extreme nationalist position and followed the policy of the Foreign Ministry, which sought a settlement with Yugoslavia. At the heart of the dispute was the city of Fiume, which had been contested for at the Paris Peace Conference, had been occupied between September 1919 and December 1920 by D'Annunzio's volunteers, and which finally became an autonomous city under terms of the Rapallo Pact of November 1920. This treaty between Italy and Yugoslavia involved Italy's abandonment of its claim to most of Dalmatia (except for Zara and the island of Lagosta) and part of the territory of Fiume (Porto Baross and the Delta) in exchange for an autonomous Fiume, attached to Italy by a land corridor. The Nationalist right cried sellout, but the treaty was supported by Mussolini, whose primary aim in 1920 was to eliminate D'Annunzio as a potential rival. Despite support for the Rapallo Treaty, the Fascists were generally hostile to the rights of Slavic minorities in Italy, so that, when Mussolini arrived in power, there were no real indicators of the direction his new government might take.

In 1923, when Fascist Italy found itself embroiled in a conflict with Greece over Albania and Corfu, relations with Yugoslavia improved to the point that both sides agreed to a new treaty for Fiume in January

1924. Italy was finally allowed to annex the city in exchange for the disputed Porto Baross and the Delta. The resolution of the Fiume issue was followed on January 27, 1924, by a treaty of friendship and cooperation between the two countries. This agreement represented a victory for those who argued that Italy had much to gain by cultivating good relations with Yugoslavia as a step toward commercial penetration in the Balkans. However, the breakthrough was never exploited. Instead, Italy and Yugoslavia drifted apart over rivalry in Albania, where in 1925 they found themselves on opposite sides in the civil war between supporters of Fan Noli, backed by Italy, and Ahmed Zogu, a Yugoslav protégé. When the latter won, it seemed that the Italians had lost ground, but the endless complexities of Balkan politics and the lure of Italian money led Zogu to break from Yugoslavia. On November 27, 1926, Italy signed a treaty with Albania that created a semiprotectorate over that country. The Yugoslavs then drew closer to their allies in the Little Entente.

The Little Entente, an alliance system formed in 1921 between Yugoslavia, Czechoslovakia, and Rumania to oppose Hungarian efforts to regain territories lost as a result of World War I, was the centerpiece of the French status quo bloc in Danubian Europe. The pivotal country in this regional grouping was Czechoslovakia. Italy at first took a neutral stand toward the Little Entente and even signed a commercial accord with Czechoslovakia in May 1924. Relations with Rumania were also friendly, so that until 1925 there seemed to be no reason to believe that Fascist policy would take a serious revisionist direction. Italy's deteriorating relationship with Yugoslavia upset all calculations. Against the advice of his own Foreign Ministry, Mussolini was drawn into a policy that aimed at surrounding Yugoslavia and, indirectly, the Little Entente, by a countersystem that included Albania, Bulgaria, and Hungary. The cornerstone of this anti-Versailles bloc was laid in a ten-year friendship pact with Hungary, signed on April 5, 1927.

Balance Sheet for the Twenties

That little of substance was achieved during the twenties by Fascist diplomacy was largely because of the inability of Italy to exploit the balance of power. Neither cordial relations with Great Britain nor cool relations with France won for Italy any real advantages. In dealing with Yugoslavia, Mussolini sought petty gains in Albania and ignored the advantages in trade and influence that might have been secured by better relations with the Yugoslavs. Instead, Italy forced Yugoslavia into closer reliance on the Little Entente and on France. In compensation, Italy gained the dubious advantage of a favored position in Albania and the potential sponsorship of a bloc of revisionist losers in World War I. Only on the Austrian issue was Mussolini decidedly antirevisionist.

In colonial matters the balance sheet was even less positive. The resurgence of modern Turkey ruled out colonies in Asia Minor. The eventual plum in Africa was Ethiopia, which Italy had failed to conquer in 1896 and still coveted to round out her East African empire, but conditions in the 1920s were not ripe for a move into Ethiopia. Italy was forced to sponsor Ethiopian membership in the League of Nations in 1923 and to sign a treaty of friendship with the African monarchy in 1928 merely to maintain her influence.

Other examples of Italian policy during this period reveal the same mixed results. Italy was technically the first of the victorious powers to recognize the USSR on February 7, 1924, when a commercial accord was signed, yet few economic opportunities materialized. The same could be said of Italian participation in the Locarno Pact of 1925, which guaranteed the Belgian-French-German border. Mussolini's efforts to extend these guarantees to the Brenner frontier with Austria met with a wall of silence.

Fascism and the Crisis of the Versailles System, 1929–34

The era of economic crisis from 1929 to 1934 restricted even further the horizons of Fascist diplomacy. From September 1929 to July 1932, Mussolini relinquished the Foreign Ministry to Dino Grandi. Enormous budget deficits forced cuts in government expenditures, including those for the military. Grandi understood that Italy lacked the means for an arms race, although later, when the country still lacked the means, Mussolini disregarded these same limitations. But in 1929 the need to go slow by was reflected in Grandi's support for disarmament and for cooperation within the framework of the League of Nations. He also sought to counter French predominance by aligning Italy more closely with England. The major achievement of this policy came at the London Naval Conference of 1930, when agreement for parity with France in warships and aircraft carriers was attained.

The rise of the Nazi movement and the inability of Italian diplomacy to make a substantial breakthrough in its campaign to play England off against France increased Mussolini's frustration with Grandi. In July 1932 Mussolini took back leadership of the Foreign Ministry and carried out a massive shift of Italian diplomatic personnel, as if to signal that Italy was no longer as committed to policies that would appeal to London or that would be compatible with the League of Nations. Henceforth, Mussolini tried to play the German card more aggressively, and, consequently, his policies took on a more personal, even ideological, cast.

The new direction in policy was unveiled in the proposal for the Four Power Pact. Mussolini longed to become the arbiter of the European balance of power. In January 1933, the new Hitler government seemed to offer a chance to pursue that goal and at the same time to meet the threat of increased ideological competition from the Nazis. By sponsoring Germany's right to equal participation with England, France, and Italy, Mussolini attempted to carve out for himself the role of mediator. The original proposal for a four-power directorate was made on March 4, 1933. It called for gradual arms parity between the Versailles powers and Germany and for cooperation among the four powers on European and colonial problems. The plan met with a lukewarm response from the British and Germans and a hailstorm of criticism from the French and their eastern European allies, who gutted the pact of any practical substance before it was signed, almost as an afterthought, in July 1933.

Austria Between Italy and Germany

By then, however, events in Germany and Austria began to alter Italian perspectives. Although Italy's relationship with Vienna had been cool during the twenties, the growth of nazism frightened the conservative Catholic leadership of Austria. Italy's chief source of support within Austria came from the Heimwehren, a paramilitary force led by Prince Ernest von Starhemberg. When Engelbert Dollfuss became chancellor of Austria in May 1932, Starhemberg's movement supported the new government. Dollfuss was an authoritarian conservative and a former minister of agriculture, who was reputed to be an expert in financial matters. Fear of the Nazis and fierce antisocialism led Dollfuss to choose Italy as the best defense of Austrian independence. Backed by Mussolini, the Austrian chancellor outlawed the Nazi party in 1933, and then in the spring of 1934, crushed the Austrian Socialist party.

At first Dollfuss's gamble seemed to pay off. The Italians made the status of Austria the test of relations with the new German government. Mussolini had maintained relations with the German right since the early twenties, but the question of the German minority in the Italian Tyrol presented a serious obstacle to cooperation with the German nationalists. In the case of Hitler, however, the situation was quite different. As early as 1928, he had made it clear to the Italians that the Nazis would not raise the issue of the Tyrol against Italy. Nonetheless, Mussolini was in no hurry to meet Hitler after January 1933. When the first encounter finally did take place in June 1934, it did not go well. Hitler appeared almost "Chaplinesque" in his business suit next to the Duce in full uniform and medals. More important, no accord between the dictators was reached on Austria, which Hitler, an Austrian by birth, sought to incorporate into the German sphere of influence. Relations reached a nadir on July 25, 1934, with the assassination of Dollfuss, just after he had finally heeded Mussolini's advice and established under Italian protection a Catholic, corporative, and authoritarian state on May 1, 1934. The Duce moved troops to the Brenner frontier and ignored German protestations of innocence.

Italian-French relations improved in direct proportion to the increased tension with Germany. Italy's preoccupation with Austria was matched by French concerns about Nazi inroads in central Europe after the stipulation of a nonaggression treaty between Germany and Poland in January 1934. Even the murder of the French foreign minister Louis Barthou and King Alexander of Yugoslavia by Croatian terrorists on the Italian payroll did not impede the thaw in relations, which took the concrete form of a joint declaration on September 27, 1934, in favor of Austrian independence.

Ethiopia

Despite the Austrian crisis, 1934 seemed promising. International conditions had finally matured for the long-awaited move into Ethiopia. To some extent, Italy's situation then paralleled her conquest of Libya in 1911. Like Libya at the time, Ethiopia was the last available territory. As before, Italy attempted to ensure the disinterest of the other powers. In both cases the international diplomatic situation provided the key for the timing of the move. Finally, like the move into Libya, which seemed unimportant in itself, the Italian attack on Ethiopia set off a chain reaction that led to general war.

The balance of power between Germany and the Versailles powers set the timetable for Fascist calculations. German rearmament was underway, but it was not far enough along to pose an immediate threat to Italy's interests in Austria. A rapid, victorious war in Africa would still leave Italy free to meet an eventual German move against Austria. Moreover, rising German power made France more willing to pay the price in Ethiopia in order to bring Italy into the camp of the status quo powers.

Several factors made a colonial war in Ethiopia different from the Libyan war, however. Ethiopia was a member of the League of Nations and entitled to protection in case of Italian aggression. Naked imperialism, such as Italy proposed, ran counter to powerful currents in international public opinion. The "Peace Ballot" of 1935 showed overwhelming support for collective security in Britain, whose support for the operation was vital. Moreover, there were no compelling internal economic imperatives in Italy for expansion in 1934 and 1935. The worst crisis of the depression had been overcome. The reorganization of the system of economic fiefdoms had been completed. Possibilities for Italian economic expansion in central Europe and in the Balkans were adequate for the limited capacities of Italian industry, although there was support for expansion in Africa from textile, mining, and construction firms.

Motivations for war must be sought elsewhere. Mussolini had by 1934 exhausted his margin for internal initiative. The function of fascism had become essentially conservative. Little that was spectacular could be achieved in such a regime without offending one or another of the powerful constituencies that fascism had institutionalized. Corporativism reached a limit with the reform of 1934. The great domestic "battles" of the 1920s had been exhausted for their propaganda value. Only the cult of the Duce remained, but its voracious appetite required constant feeding. Mussolini well understood the powerful undercurrent of support among Italians for "poor people's imperialism"—the idea that Italy, a poor and overpopulated nation, had a right to colonies—and that that support could be mobilized behind the Ethiopian war. Finally, there was an economic dimension; although there was no economic necessity for war in 1934, favored special interests were not necessarily hostile to expansion.

An incident on December 5, 1934, along the undefined border between Italian Somalia and Ethiopia offered Mussolini his pretext. The Italians rejected all efforts at mediation of the dispute called for under terms of the 1928 treaty. Obviously, Mussolini believed that French and British opposition would be minimal. A Franco-Italian accord of January 1935 confirmed this view. Both powers pledged support for the status quo in Austria and in the Balkans. France made a minor border concession in favor of Libya and Eritrea, and the Italians made a major gesture by agreeing to the progressive liquidation of Italian minority rights in Tunisia. The Fascists claimed that their generosity was prompted by secret assurances about Ethiopia from Foreign Minister Pierre Laval, although Laval contended unconvincingly that he meant only economic rights. Ethiopia was not mentioned at the Stresa Conference between Italy, Great Britain, and France, held in April 1935. At that time, the three powers agreed on the maintenance of the status quo in central Europe. When Mussolini's stand that the communiqué should refer only to Europe met with no objection, he took the omission to imply consent to the Italian conquest. Eventually, the British half-heartedly clarified their position by sending Anthony Eden to Rome in May to offer a deal whereby Ethiopia's Ogaden region would pass to Italy and Britain would compensate Ethiopia with an outlet to the sea. Mussolini rejected the offer on the grounds that it amounted to a British protectorate for the remainder of Ethiopia.

War between Italy and Ethiopia broke out on October 3, 1935. On October 7, the League of Nations declared Italy the aggressor and a few days later voted sanctions. The British and French desperately sought a basis for compromise. In December British Foreign Secretary Sir Samuel Hoare and Laval offered Mussolini a large part of Ethiopia, if he would allow the fiction of a rump Ethiopian state. The Italians accepted, but the contents of the deal were leaked to the press, and public opinion killed the agreement. Sanctions were applied, but in such a manner as to be ineffective. The British refused to close the Suez Canal to Italian shipping. The League exempted petroleum products from the list of banned items, and non-League powers like the United States, Germany, and Japan refused to join the boycott. After some initial indications that the Italians might have trouble in subduing Ethiopia, Italy surged forward to capture Addis Ababa in May 1936 and proclaimed the new Italian African Empire.

Domestic Consequences of the Ethiopian War

The war won for the Fascist regime support from important sectors of society. Backing came from the Catholic hierarchy, the middle class, and even from some workers and peasants. It was a popular war during which the Fascist state reached the peak of its internal consensus. (It must be remembered, however, that consensus in a dictatorship is hard to measure.) Some of this enthusiasm was genuine; much of it was created by an extraordinary propaganda effort. During the war the Office of Press and Propaganda, which had been a mere department under the Head of Government, was elevated to cabinet status and turned over to Mussolini's son-in-law, Galeazzo Ciano. Radio, films, newspapers, and schools were used as instruments in the struggle for the hearts and minds of the population. But the war also had the negative effect of killing hopes for domestic reform. Officially billed as a "pause" in the construction of the corporative order, the outbreak of war ended any serious initiatives in that direction. Finally, the conquest of Ethiopia marked the first steps toward Fascist racism when a code of conduct was promulgated to regulate sexual and social contacts between Africans and Italians. No longer were Nazi ideology and race-thinking scorned by intelligent Fascists. After 1935, the regime's propagandists tended to emphasize the common ground between the two movements.

Part Three
The Downward Spiral
1935–45

Chapter Seven
Fascism at War: Economy and Society 1935–43

From 1935 to the outbreak of World War II there were no major innovations in Fascist economic thinking. Earlier trends and policies were merely accentuated. The Fascist regime left agriculture in private hands but exercised increasingly strong controls over production targets by stockpiling important commodities. The effect of these measures was the elimination of market forces because major producers were allowed to operate in a system of state-established prices and quotas. Consumer-oriented light industry continued to suffer from discrimination in the allocation of raw materials and from lack of government support in opening new markets abroad. Finally, there was a continuing interpenetration of the state with heavy industry. The regime took an ever increasing role in the areas of banking, industrial production, and foreign trade. The two instruments of intervention were the IRI (1933) and the Superintendency of Foreign Exchange and Commerce, created in 1935.

The Fascist government, pushed by successive wars in Ethiopia, Spain, and Albania between 1935 and 1939, carried to their logical conclusion measures which had been in effect since the beginning of the depression. Foreign competition was largely eliminated from the Italian market by high tariffs and exchange controls. Carefully regulated cartelization agreements and extremely high prices eased the economic situation for key industries, which operated as virtual baronies in their sectors. An undesirable side effect of these policies was spiraling inflation after 1936.

Autarchy

As the regime prepared for war in Ethiopia in 1935, it adopted a series of measures aimed at curbing the trade deficit and the outflow of gold reserves. On February 16, 1935, controls over foreign exchange and licensing regulations for imports were tightened. In May the government established the Superintendency of Foreign Exchange and Commerce under the direction of Felice Guarneri, an official of the Confindustria, who became virtual economic czar through his control over raw material imports. Holders of foreign exchange were required to deposit it with the Bank of Italy, which allocated it to certain basic industries for the purchase of materials. The cartels, in the guise of *giunte corporative* (corporative boards), distributed the raw materials to their members. By mid-1935 the state regulated the distribution of coal, coke, tin, nickel, and copper. The imposition of sanctions by the League of Nations in October 1935 and fear of a long war led to strict conservation measures, but, even after victory in 1936, the regime continued to shape the economy along lines dictated by the war emergency. On March 23, 1936, Mussolini officially employed to term *autarchy* to define the regime's long-term goal of economic self-sufficiency as a step toward putting Italy on a permanent war footing.

The regime was able to build on its accumulated economic powers to administer that drive for self-sufficiency. A fundamental step in rounding out these powers was the Banking Reform of 1936, which severed the link between the large banks and industrial financing. The Bank of Italy, formerly a private facility, became a state institution through which the government could directly carry out its financial operations. Several levels of banking were established, with certain major banks, like the Banca Commerciale, becoming publicly owned banks of national interest. None were allowed to engage in long-term industrial financing, although short-term commercial credit was still available. The IRI took on its role (which continues to this day) as chief holding company for state participation in industry. Between 1935 and 1939, whole sectors were reorganized into subsidiary companies under the IRI: Navalmeccanica for ship construction, Finmare for shipping lines, and Finsider for steel. Through its control over these vital sectors, the regime was able to coordinate allied sectors, such as rubber, chemicals, and electricity, which remained in private hands.

Import Substitution and Cartelization

Italian dependence on imported raw materials led the Fascist regime to move in two directions. In order to increase import substitution for the goal of economic self-sufficiency, the state engaged directly in several ventures. The Azienda Generale Italiana Petroli (AGIP), created in 1926, and the Ente Nazionale del Metano explored for oil and natural gas in Albania, Sicily, and the Po Valley. Coal production was put under the direction of the Azienda Carboni Italiani. Strategic metals, like copper, tin, and nickel, were under the control of the Azienda Minerali Metalli Italiani. The regime also entered into joint ventures with privileged industrial giants. Such was the case in the development of synthetic fuels by the Azienda Nazionale Idrogenazione Combustibili in which the state participated along with Montecatini, the major chemical firm. Similar cooperative efforts were carried out for the production of explosives, paper, and rayon. The results of these ventures in autarchy are difficult to determine. The cost of import substitution was extremely high. Synthetic rubber cost four times the price of natural rubber, and Italian coal was far more costly than English coal. Although some gains were made in certain areas, like electrification, autarchy involved a dispersion of scarce resources.

Under autarchy, control of Italian basic industry was centralized even further. By 1939, IRI controlled 77 percent of pig iron production, 45 percent of steel, 80 percent of naval construction, and 90 percent of shipping. Fiat dominated auto production; two or three firms did the same for the electrical industry. A major chemical giant like Montecatini was an empire unto itself, comprising 43 smaller firms, 188 plants, and 64,000 workers. Along with the SNIA Viscosa, it totally controlled the chemical industry.

The leadership of these firms was closely integrated into a veritable military-industrial complex with the major figures of industry and the armed forces shifting back and forth between high government positions and the private sector. While there were growing doubts among some industrialists about the wisdom of such a close relationship, especially as the drift in foreign policy carried Italy too far into the German camp, the cost of reversing the system was beyond the means of any single industrialist or even the Confindustria itself. Heavy industry had too great a stake in the existing system to rebel against it. Supposedly safe in their fiefdoms, the industrialists found themselves with less and less control over the main lines of Fascist foreign policy, even as they became more preoccupied by certain aspects of the regime.

A Permanent War Economy?

The decision to go to war over Ethiopia was not in itself an irretrievable choice for the regime. The stress put on the economic system might have been relieved by a return to peace after 1936, but this was not to be the case. The war in Ethiopia upset the balance of power that had restrained Nazi Germany. Henceforth, external events would press Italy further down the road indicated by its involvement in Ethiopia. Economic measures were hastily improvised to suit the needs of foreign policy. Because of the shift in interest to the Mediterranean, carefully built-up markets in eastern Europe were sacrificed. Permanent war increased public spending and budget deficits, which ballooned from two to sixteen billion lire between 1934 and 1937. Prices at home skyrocketed. Despite Mussolini's attachment to the overvalued lira, its low exchange rate could no longer be maintained after successive devaluations of the other major currencies. In late 1936 the government faced the inevitable and announced a 40 percent devaluation. Still, prices continued to rise, and the regime was forced to impose price controls in 1936 and to allow general wage increases in 1936 and 1937.

Mass Mobilization

Throughout the twenties, when there had been some possibility of restoring traditional structures both at home and abroad, the Fascist regime moved naturally within an authoritarian, conservative context. Beginning in 1929, several things happened. The depression created the possibility of social unrest and the need to channel opinion to accept wage reductions and other sacrifices. While the regime still respected its basic compromises, the government was forced to become involved more deeply in the workings of the economy. The compartmentalization of the regime into separate fiefdoms made it difficult for any one interest group to influence policy outside of its defined sphere. Most conspicuous in this regard was foreign policy, where Mussolini found increasing freedom. Important groups within the Fascist system grossly underestimated how the deterioration of the European order subverted the basis of earlier political and institutional restraints on Mussolini (pressures from the Foreign Office and the limitations of the balance of power), and how this freedom in the area of foreign policy in turn created further opportunities to alter the domestic political framework. The fiefdoms—Church, military, industry—considered their power secure as long as they could maintain control over their own narrowly defined interests, but they disregarded the major changes that were taking place in the way public life was conducted.

Competition from Nazi Germany added yet another volatile element. Equality for Germany within the European system opened new foreign policy options for Italy but exposed the country to much greater risks as well. We have already seen how the new freedom had an effect on Mussolini's calculations with regard to the Four Power Pact and the Ethiopian war. Growing German power both frightened and fascinated the Duce, whose opportunistic nature was attracted by successful displays of naked power.

The Nazis also profoundly disrupted the Fascist sense of security. The political and ideological dynamism of nazism challenged the smug superiority of the Fascists, who had initially regarded Hitler as no more than a poor copy of Mussolini. Despite the fact that the Fascists had pioneered the instruments of totalitarian rule—the single party, the paramilitary squads, terror, the use of propaganda to mobilize the masses—the regime was ensnarled in its compromises with the conservative order. Nowhere was this more apparent than in the field of mass propaganda and mass mobilization, where, by contrast, the

Nazis excelled. Here the authoritarian political managers had great leverage, yet Fascist mobilization remained a little-felt, superficial phenomenon. The conviction and the vision, so frighteningly present in Nazi propaganda, were missing in Fascist Italy, in part because the propaganda apparatus operated in the context of a government that was mired in bureaucratic routine and that discouraged dramatic initiatives. Thus, as public confidence in the Fascist government dwindled after the temporary enthusiasm over Ethiopia, the response from the mass of Italians became increasingly passive. Fascist efforts to regulate private conduct brought ridicule, as in the case of the annoying effort to abolish the formal *lei* (you) term of address (judged foreign and effeminate) and its substitution of *voi*; or defiance, when the regime intervened in the private lives of the Italians with exhortations to bear more children; or shame, over discrimination against the Jews.

Mass Organizations in the 1930s

The PNF should have been the instrument of mass mobilization. On paper it was a formidible organization of 2,500,000 members in 1939, but many belonged merely as a condition of employment. What had begun as an unruly band of vigilantes in 1920 now became a vast, bureaucratic apparatus with a rigid hierarchy, from the local *fiduciario*, to the provincial *federale*, to the secretary of the PNF and the Duce. For years the party's internal critics had warned that life was being drained out of the party by its all-pervasive authoritarianism, yet Starace made no effort to rejuvenate it. When he was finally replaced in late 1939, it was by a series of political lightweights: Ettore Muti, a war hero whose medals gave him the title of "the most beautiful bosom in Italy"; Adelchi Serena, a government minister of no prestige; and Aldo Vidussoni, an extraordinarily limited young man who was hailed as the "best" in Fascist youth. It was as if no one was in charge. The diaries of Galeazzo Ciano and Giuseppe Bottai and Curzio Malaparte's *Kaputt* leave a vivid account of the petty bickering and cynicism which gripped Italian society before the war.

Living Conditions

The standard of living for the masses of Italians probably worsened in significant ways between 1929 and 1939, although this was a general phenomenon in all industrial societies. This decline was certainly true for the peasants and unskilled workers, as well as for the relatively privileged industrial workers. Hourly wages and monthly earnings in industry declined rapidly between 1927 and 1935 under the impact of government-forced wage cuts. At the same time, the cost-of-living index dropped, so that monthly earnings in industry (taking account of cuts in hours) kept slightly ahead of the cost of living between 1932 and 1934. Despite wage increases of over 30 percent, the cost of living increased so rapidly between 1936 and 1939 that workers actually lost ground in terms of real monthly earnings. The average hours worked per month declined from 182 in 1929, to 172 in 1934, to 160 in 1939. Thus, the introduction of a forty-hour week for some workers in 1934 represented a wage cut. Unemployment remained quite high as well. It dropped below 1 million in 1934 and to 700,000 in the years of constant warfare after 1936, but these figures were far above those of the predepression years.

Fascist labor leaders found their position almost impossible during the thirties. Not only did they have to accept and transmit to the workers the mandated salary cuts, but they were unable to protect the workers from discriminatory practices, such as job reclassification at lower pay. Therefore the unions tended to compensate by concentrating their demands on fringe benefits, which the regime was willing to grant in collective contracts. In this way several important social benefits were passed down: family subsidies in 1934, sick pay increases from 1928 to 1938, year-end bonuses in 1938, paid national holidays in 1938. Health insurance was gradually extended, although most job-related illnesses received little or no coverage.

These fringe benefits, rather than wages, had advantages from the standpoint of the regime. They partially made up for wage cuts without encouraging consumption in a period of autarchy. For instance, family subsidies, introduced in 1934 along with the forty-hour week, were intended to ease the burden which the cutback in working time put on the wage earner. At the same time, the family subsidies had, as the main aim, the encouragement of large families.

Women, Work, and Family

The demographic program, more than any concern for the workers, accounted for the expansion of many social benefits. The origins of the program to increase the population went back to the 1920s but received renewed emphasis with the outbreak of the Ethiopian war. The motivations were quite complex. Fascist theorists equated declining birthrates, as in France, with an overall crisis of national vitality. They felt that large families in rural areas would counterbalance the tendency toward reduced birthrates in cities and would stabilize the social structure. By necessity, larger families would force women to return to their traditional roles. To these considerations were added three others after the Ethiopian war. The Fascists felt that the increased population could and should be absorbed by their new empire. Moreover, the era of renewed warfare demanded an increased supply of young men. Finally, the Fascists were attracted by the aspect of totalitarian engineering and massification of the existing population that the demographic program offered.

Several important consequences stemmed from the active promotion of large families. Subsidies, begun in 1934 for the second child, were extended to the first infant in 1935. Special taxes on single people, marriage loans, and preference in employment to fathers of large families were introduced.

The regime's emphasis on large families also led the government to take a more negative stand on women's rights. Ironically, fascism's 1919–20 programs had offered women the vote and a promise of social equality, but the close identification of the Fascist movement with the veterans led to a sharp reversal of position. The Fascists became ardent supporters of preferences for former soldiers and accepted discrimination against women who had entered the work force between 1911 and 1918. As might be expected from the degree of male lower-middle-class support for fascism, the Mussolini government was especially hard on white-collar and professional women. The first minister of public instruction, Gentile, restricted the rights of women to teach in certain predominately male upper-level schools and in certain subject matters, like philosophy. The Fascist government made no effort to repeal restrictions on women in the legal profession, and, despite earlier promises and pressure from women's organizations, the government hedged on commitments to bring a women's suffrage bill to parliament. Mussolini finally did allow women to vote in local elections, but, almost simultaneously, in 1926, the government abandoned democratic local administration.

The depression brought a spate of laws further curbing work for women. Preference was given to men in public employment, and in 1933 new regulations limited the rights of women to compete in state examinations. The social legislation of the 1930s had the effect of increasing the cost of female labor. As if this were not enough, a law passed in 1938 restricted females to no more than 10 percent of the work force in private and state enterprises, and a 1939 decree defined certain areas of "female" labor where percentages might rise higher—typists, clerks, telephone operators, and the like. Timid attempts by university-educated women to defend professional career choices were halted around 1934. Instead, procreation and child rearing were set forth as the exclusive functions of all women. There was even a "Day of the Mother and Child" proclaimed in 1933. Major programs were launched under the auspices of the Opera Nazionale Maternità ed Infanzia to provide medical care, to distribute milk, and to offer other assistance to mothers and small children. The regime in its lucid moments was aware that the high rate of infant mortality was a major depressant on population growth. Yet, despite all these efforts, the birthrate declined. In the 1921–25 period, there were 29.9 live births per thousand; by the years 1936–40, this figure had fallen to 23.1. Birthrates for Turin and Milan were comparable to those in modern European and American cities.

Fascist Racial Policies

The closer relationship between Italy and Germany after 1936 coincided with ominous developments within Italy over racial policy.

Unlike nazism, Italian fascism had never put race at the center of its ideology. The core of fascism was extreme nationalism. Mussolini's own position toward Italian Jews had never been openly hostile. Several of his close collaborators, and one of his most famous mistresses, Margherita Sarfatti, were Jewish, and important Fascist leaders, like Italo Balbo, had strong ties to their local Jewish communities. Mussolini even reluctantly tolerated some Zionist activity in Italy, which led to the formation of an Italy-Palestine Committee in 1928. In his famous interview with Emil Ludwig in 1930, Mussolini expressed contempt for biological racism. Like other groups, large and small, the Italian Jews were granted their own semiautonomous status. Between October 1930 and November 1931, as a result of the status given to Catholicism as state religion in the Lateran Treaty, the Jewish community became an officially recognized and tolerated religious body under a central administration, the Union of Italian Jewish Communities.

While there was no fundamental discrimination against Italian Jews, Mussolini left no doubt that he would not tolerate competition with fascism's own extreme nationalism. Conflict never arose, however, because Italian Jews were indistinguishable from the rest of the population in their attitude toward the regime. The relatively benign situation did not mean that Italy lacked rabid anti-Semites, such as Giovanni Preziosi, the editor of *Vita Italiana*, and Telesio Interlandi, whose Roman newspaper *Il Tevere* was occasionally used by Mussolini as an unofficial vehicle. These Nazi-like racists were joined by numerous opportunists or supporters of the German alliance, like Farinacci (whose anti-Semitism was designed primarily to cement the alliance with Hitler and who "Aryanized" his Jewish private secretary for the duration).

The Nazi seizure of power initially failed to shake Italian wariness concerning racial prejudice. Instead, Nazi doctrines provoked Italian Fascists to stress the universality of their traditions, which excluded no part of the national community on grounds of blood or physical characteristics. Traditionally, the Fascists had understood "race policy" in terms of demographic measures to increase the population and ruralization. The alteration in outlook first came during the Ethiopian war in a classic example of the connection between imperialism and racism. The first elements of an emerging racial consciousness were applied to the Africans. Mussolini even stated that empire was impossible without race consciousness, presumably to increase feelings of superiority among the conquerors.

After 1936 the shifting diplomatic balance allowed the new climate of European race-thinking to work on Italian fascism. The Fascists were not necessarily copying the Germans, but they were certainly responding to what was perceived as increased ideological and political competition from Germany. It was easy to broaden the elements in Fascist ideology, such as extreme and exclusive nationalism, and those which dealt with the role of women and the need for a higher birthrate, traditional areas of *la politica della razza* (race policy), to measures that served to protect a supposedly pure Italian race from various forms of "contagion" from other races. It was not merely by chance that medical and demographic experts on policy toward women expressed their ideas in notoriously anti-Semitic journals like Interlandi's *Difesa della Razza*.

The campaign against the Jews began in July 1938 with the publication, under the auspices of the Ministry of Popular Culture, of a "Manifesto of Fascist Racism." In September a government decree limited the rights of foreign Jews to live in Italy and revoked the citizenship granted to foreign-born Jews after January 1, 1919. It was followed on September 2 by a law banning Jewish students and teachers from the schools (although converted Jews could still attend Catholic schools). Special Jewish schools were established. In October the Grand Council banned Jews from the PNF and forbade mixed marriages. Jews were also purged from all cultural, professional, and academic associations. They were not allowed to own land or to operate businesses that employed more than one hundred persons. Finally, the Law for the Defense of the Race formalized the ban on mixed marriages. War veterans, their families, some early members of the PNF, and children of mixed marriages who did not profess the Jewish religion were excluded from some of these provisions, although the regime ran into difficulties with the Catholic Church over the ban on mixed marriages. Priests were not allowed by the Church to refuse marriage to converted Jews, but after October 1938, the state refused to recognize the civil effects of these religious ceremonies. The various "imperfections" outraged the hard-line anti-Semites, but they did not spare thousands of Italians, who, like the characters in Giorgio Bassani's *The Garden of the Finzi-Contini* (1962), had their careers and lives disrupted or destroyed.

Chapter Eight
The Reorientation
of Foreign Policy
1936–43

Italian Diplomacy at the Crossroads

The end of the Ethiopian war brought on the last major governmental reorganization before the outbreak of World War II. The changes that took place on June 11, 1936, marked the emergence of a new generation of Fascist leaders, but, significantly, this last government before the war was singularly devoid of major domestic policy initiatives. Except for the school reform, associated with Minister of National Education Bottai, domestic policy functioned merely as a coda to Fascist diplomacy. The most important member of the new government was Galeazzo Ciano, who assumed control of the Foreign Ministry. Ciano's career was a textbook case of success under fascism. He was the son of Costanzo Ciano, a war hero, businessman from Livorno, and old associate of Mussolini. The younger Ciano was extremely bright, but also frivolous and superficial—a dangerous combination in later years when it led him to overestimate his abilities and underestimate the advantages of patient preparation. After an abortive career as a dramatist and journalist, Ciano entered the diplomatic corps. His style and good looks won him a series of mistresses and finally the attention of Mussolini's favorite daughter, Edda, who was equally young and headstrong, a notorious gambler, and who had her own stable of past and present lovers. For Ciano it was a match that made his career. A series of rapid promotions saw him move from the foreign service, to the head of the Press Office, to minister of press and propaganda before becoming foreign minister in 1936. But success had its price. Ciano had

no real following in the country and was totally dependent on Mussolini. The cruel joke that circulated in Rome expressed it well. When
asked if Ciano could do anything well, the response was that, of course,
he was an excellent cuckold. But no, on second thought, even there he
needed his wife's help. On Ciano's shoulders would fall much of the
responsibility for the pivotal decisions made between 1936 and 1939.

The Spanish Civil War was a turning point for Fascist foreign policy.
Up to the end of the Ethiopian conflict Italian diplomacy had shown
continuity with the past, even if the execution of policy was often more
aggressive than diplomatic traditionalists might have liked. It was
anchored on friendship with England and on the desire to maintain a
balance between German and French power on the Continent. While
the country was engaged in Ethiopia, Hitler remilitarized the Rhine-
land. The movement in March 1936 of German troops up to the border
of France and Belgium destroyed the French strategic advantage won
in the Versailles Treaty and made French intervention in defense of its
eastern European allies much more difficult. As a result, Austria became almost totally dependent on Italy for protection.

Three decisions became paramount for the Fascist government as the
war in Ethiopia wound down. First, there was the question of the
compatibility between Italy's semiprotectorate over Austria and a developing relationship with Nazi Germany, its major rival for influence
in Austria. Second, Italy faced the problem of repairing its relationship
with France and England. Third, the Italians had to take a stand on the
military revolt that broke out in July 1936 against the Spanish Republican government. Mussolini and Ciano resolved these three choices in
ways that marked a major break with the past and had profound
consequences for both domestic and foreign policy.

Italy, Austria, and Germany in 1936

One of the casualties of the governmental change in Italy was the
undersecretary at the Foreign Ministry, Fulvio Suvich, a native of
Trieste, who had a strong interest in Austrian and Danubian affairs.
Suvich's departure coincided with Mussolini's warning to Austria on
June 6, 1936, that it should negotiate with Hitler. The result was the

Austro-German accord of July, which acknowledged Austria's status as a German state. Simultaneously, the Germans moved to assure the Italians that they were willing to recognize the Italian empire in Ethiopia. These moves culminated in a meeting between Ciano and Hitler on October 21 and 22, 1936, at which an agreement between the two countries was worked out. Its major provisions involved coordination of policy on Spain and the League of Nations, Italian recognition of the Austro-German accord of July, and German recognition of the Italian conquest of Ethiopia. This pact, dubbed by Mussolini the "Axis" around which European politics would revolve, was neither a political nor a military alliance. The tilt toward Nazi Germany should not be underestimated, however, because, while no fundamental issue separated Italy and England, bitterness over Ethiopia persisted, and relations with France were at a new low after the victory in May 1936 of the French Popular Front brought to power an alliance of radicals, socialists, and communists.

Italian Intervention in the Spanish Civil War

The war in Spain became the test of future Fascist policy. Italian involvement with the Spanish right went back to 1932, when the Fascists encouraged the anti-Republican military revolt of General José Sanjurjo. In March 1934, Mussolini and Italo Balbo received a delegation of Spanish monarchists and promised arms to the anti-Republican opposition. Despite these early contacts, the Italians did not participate in the planning for the revolt in July 1936, but the Fascist regime was immediately confronted by an urgent request for air and naval support from General Francisco Franco in North Africa.

The Italian decision to intervene was a political and strategic error, motivated by hostility toward the French and the Spanish Popular Front governments, by vague plans for expanded influence in the Mediterranean region, and by fears of Soviet penetration in Spain. There was nothing even particularly "fascist" about Italy's intervention, since Mussolini did not consistently aim at the creation of a Fascist state there. Eventually, the Italians poured 72,000 men and well over 5,000 officers into the Spanish conflict. As time wore on, this commitment needlessly involved the prestige of the regime. For their efforts on behalf of the Spanish rebels the Italians received remarkably little in return. The treaty of November 1936, which governed relations between Fascist Italy and Franco's Nationalists, offered Italy nothing but a promise of Spain's neutrality in the event of war with a third power. The war meant that Italy was never able to turn back to the Danubian Basin, as Mussolini had planned when he began the Ethiopian venture. An aggressive Mediterranean policy increased conflicts with France and made good relations with England more difficult. The intervention in Spain forced Italy to coordinate policy more closely with Nazi Germany, which joined in aiding the Spanish rebels. Finally, intervention revealed a reckless quality in Italian diplomacy. Unlike Germany, which drove a hard bargain for aid, the Italians offered much, obtained little, and seemed unsure of what they wanted. The fatal tendency to allow policy to be set by a more aggressive and resolute partner would recur in Italy's relationship with Germany.

Even the short-term economic gains for Italy were minimal. Unemployment, which threatened to rise in 1937, was reduced by another military engagement. Key industries, Fiat, for example, reaped profits from dealings with Spain because credit was provided by the government, which minimized any risk of default. But, even in the area of trade, negatives predominated. From 1930 on, Italy had made a determined effort to build markets in eastern Europe. Clearing agreements had been worked out with Hungary, Rumania, Bulgaria, and Yugoslavia in 1929. The growing friendship between Italy, Hungary, and Austria was underscored by commercial accords in 1932 and by a bilateral Italo-Austrian agreement in 1934. Important contracts, strongly backed by the Fascist regime, were signed between Fiat and the Polish and Soviet governments. These positions, however, were challenged after 1933 by Germany, which aggressively entered the Danubian and Balkan markets. During the Ethiopian war the imposition of economic sanctions harmed Italian interests in eastern Europe, and the intervention in Spain delivered the coup de grace to Italy's position in the Balkans. In the end, the war did not even serve as a stimulus to further Italian rearmament. Italy did not replace rapidly enough the weapons expended, nor did the regime work with a sense of urgency to overcome the defects that were revealed in many of the weapons used. Because the bulk of the aid to Spain was given in 1936 and 1937, there would have been ample time to overcome these deficiencies before World War II.

Italy Between Nazi Germany and the West, 1937–39

Italian involvement in Spain meant that the Italians no longer had the freedom of maneuver to defend its Austrian satellite. Time had run out for Austria. Italy accepted the July 1936 accord between Germany and Austria and specifically recognized the German sphere of interest in the Axis agreement of October. When Mussolini formally declared in November 1937 that the center of gravity of Italian policy was the Mediterranean Sea, Italy sought only to delay the moment when Germany would crush Austria. Total humiliation was barely spared the Italians. Mussolini received notice of Hitler's intent to move into Austria on March 11, 1938, only hours before the invasion. The German seizure of Austria left Italy with a feeling of defeat that even Fascist propaganda could not conceal. In one stroke, most of the strategic gains of World War I were lost.

Fear of war dictated Italy's conduct during the Munich crisis of September 1938 when Nazi Germany threatened war to detach the Sudetenland from Czechoslovakia. What little the Italians learned of Hitler's plans for Czechoslovakia came from the Italian ambassador in Berlin, Bernardo Attolico (an opponent of total subservience to German interests after his initial enthusiasm for the Axis cooled), rather than from their German "friends." Mussolini's successful proposal for mediation, which led to the meeting of the British, French, Germans, and Italians at Munich, gave the Duce unexpected fame as peacemaker, although the Italian role at the conference was marginal.

After Munich, Mussolini found himself closer than ever to the Germans, but he still had the sense to refuse Ribbentrop's overtures for a direct alliance. His options were limited, however, by his stubborn refusal to improve relations with France and England after the end of the Spanish Civil War in March 1939. Rather than using Italy's pivotal position between the great powers, Mussolini and Ciano bumbled into the "Pact of Steel" of May 22, 1939. This concession to Germany's demand for a formal military alliance was made without the Fascists even defining specific Italian objectives to be included in the treaty. The essence of the treaty involved a broadly worded promise of mutual support should one of the partners become involved in a conflict. The Italians were lulled by German assurances that they had no intention of an immediate war. Incredibly, Ciano worked from a German draft that gave Hitler carte blanche for a war of aggression. The most Italy was able to do in these months was to profit from the confusion caused by Hitler's policies to move into Albania in April 1939.

Throughout the summer of 1939, the Italians seemed unaware of the scope of Germany's plans for Poland and were told nothing of the negotiations between Nazi Germany and the USSR, which culminated in the Molotov-Ribbentrop treaty of August 23. News of the agreement shocked the Italians. Spurred on by the Italian ambassador Attolico in Berlin and his German counterpart in Rome, Georg von Mackensen, a thoroughly terrified Ciano frantically submitted to Germany a list of vital materials which, as he nicely put it, would choke a horse, if a horse could read. The Germans offered only a fraction of the supplies requested, and Italy, in a painful reminder of the earlier decision not to go to war in August 1914, declared its neutrality on September 3, 1939.

As if to emphasize the decision against war, Mussolini orchestrated a vast governmental reorganization at the end of 1939, which increased the power of the group around Ciano in favor of neutrality. Practically every major position was changed except for Ciano, Bottai (Education), and Thaon Di Revel (Finance). A separate, but important, change that occurred at almost the same time was the appointment of Carmine Senise as chief of police (succeeding the late Arturo Bocchini, who had held the post since 1926). Senise, like Bocchini, was a career bureaucrat whose loyalties were divided between the regime and the monarchy—a fact that would become important during the final days of the regime. Although the new government reflected the temporary ascendancy of Ciano's neutralist position, the cabinet had no collective power over policy. One of the basic tendencies during the thirties in the Italian government was the growth of ministerial irresponsibility. There was no mechanism for joint decisions. Mussolini remained the ultimate arbiter, but he was increasingly influenced by external events.

His power over foreign affairs went unchecked within the government.

Italian Fascism and World War II

After almost twenty years of Fascist rule, Italy was probably less prepared for a major conflict in 1940 than it had been in 1915. The country lagged behind in almost every category of raw materials and strategic reserves. The various war-planning bodies failed to overcome the resistance of entrenched economic and military fiefdoms. The industrialists were well aware of the problem and were generally in favor of neutrality in 1939. But Italy's position was precarious. She had lost her Balkan and continental markets to Germany and found it difficult to carry on normal trade in the face of the English naval blockade against Germany. Germany absorbed Italy's agricultural products and excess manpower. The failure of the economic policies of autarchy left the Fascist regime vulnerable to Nazi pressure. When not carried away by the euphoria of his meetings with the Führer, Mussolini was well aware that Italy was not prepared for war. He hoped that war might be delayed. When it was not, neutrality became a necessity, but it was a bitter pill for a man whose career had turned on an earlier decision to support Italy's entry into World War I.

After a period of wavering in late 1939, Mussolini met Hitler on March 18, 1940, and promised to enter the war at the opportune moment. Three weeks later, in a memorandum to Ciano and his military commanders, the Duce stressed the need for war to consolidate Italy's position in the Mediterranean. The collapse of France in June 1940 swept away all remaining doubts about the ultimate German victory. On June 10, Italy declared war on a prostrate France, yet, even here, the weaknesses of Italian diplomacy were apparent. Italy was merely reacting to events created by others, and, more important, the Fascist regime was placed in a position in which it was forced to accept German terms. Hitler thought it far more important to mollify the French in view of the forthcoming attack on Great Britain than to accede to Italian demands for Nice, Corsica, and Tunisia. Mussolini's gamble in declaring war came to rest on Germany's conquest of England. When that failed, all calculations behind the war crumbled.

The Debacle in Greece

After the summer of 1940, the Fascist government embarked on a race to carve out its own sphere in the Balkans before the Germans could become free to move in that direction. Instead of attacking British positions in Egypt, Mussolini threatened war against Yugoslavia and then declared war on Greece in October without informing his German ally. From the Italian point of view, the Greek campaign was a masterpiece of ineptitude that threatened to become a national humiliation when the Greek army won a series of major victories. Marshall Pietro Badoglio, who was made the scapegoat for the miscalculations behind the Greek campaign, was replaced as chief-of-staff by Marshall Ugo Cavallero. (Cavallero, a former director of the Ansaldo firm, was a typical example of the industrial-military complex.) Political paralysis spread to the home front when Mussolini capriciously decided to send all high officials, like Grandi, Bottai, and Ciano, to the front.

The failure of Italian arms in Greece inevitably drew German attention to the Balkans, but it was the Yugoslav gesture of heroic defiance in March 1941 by installing an anti-Nazi government that led to a full-scale German invasion of Yugoslavia and Greece. By mid-1941 the Italian position was salvaged with German help. Italy annexed part of Slovenia and occupied Montenegro and a large part of the Dalmatian coast. Despite the failure of the Axis to take Malta from the British, the war seemed to be proceeding well in Europe and in North Africa, where German intervention reversed another series of Italian defeats at the hands of the British. East Africa was another matter. There, the British quickly snuffed out. the newly won Italian Empire.

The Growing Crisis

The war put tremendous pressure on the fragile political alliances created by the regime. Lacking any central belief, except the myth of the Duce, the various fiefdoms tended to act defensively to protect their own interests. In short, the regime began to dissolve into its component parts. The Fascist party, which should have served as a unifying force for the entire system, was practically useless. It was ill-suited to deal with the war emergency, to mobilize the population, to monitor the popular mood, or to create a sense of national participation in the struggle. Its ranks had been bloated, from 2.5 million to 3.5 million members, by the inclusion of military draftees. The umbrella youth organization, the Gioventù Italiana del Littorio, grew to almost 8.5 million. Staggering under the weight of these forced memberships, the PNF could not act; it merely existed. Old party extremists were neither alienated or comfortably in office. Young reformers were either disillusioned or forced to count on the war to instill a renewed sense of mission to the regime.

If the party disintegrated, so too did the other elements of the Fascist consensus. As the war turned sour in 1942, the industrialists began to press for a separate peace. The Vatican worked to consolidate its political and social apparatus. The Church maintained a foot in both camps. It had alternative leadership in the wings: Sturzo in exile, Alcide De Gasperi and Giudo Gonella in the Vatican, Giovanni Gronchi and Achille Grandi, both former syndicalists and *Popolari*, and a growing number of Catholic participants in the Resistance. But the Vatican was also willing to facilitate any possibility of a conservative peace, even if it included elements of the old Fascist leadership.

Other components of the regime reacted in the same way. The state police force, under Senise, sought to strengthen its connection with the conservative monarchists. Dissident military leaders, led by the embittered Badoglio and Marshall Enrico Caviglia, became pivotal figures in separate plots to withdraw Italy from the war. Although the official military leadership under Cavallero was pro-Axis, failure in North Africa cost Cavallero his job, and Vittorio Ambrosio, his successor in 1943, followed a far more ambiguous line toward the military conspirators against Mussolini. The collapse of the German offensive in Russia and the victorious Anglo-American assault in North Africa in November and December 1942 destroyed any faith that Ciano had in a German victory. Except for Mussolini, who was ill for much of this time, the Fascist political and military leaders sought a way out of the war.

Toward the Meeting of the Fascist
Grand Council, July 24–25, 1943

Mussolini's fall from power minimized the rupture with the past that had occurred. It was engineered by conservatives who were motivated primarily by fear of military defeat. They had all been involved with fascism, either directly, as was the case with Dino Grandi, Giuseppe Bottai, or Luigi Federzoni, or as fellow travelers, as in the case of the monarchists, industrialists, and military leaders who had been the core of hyphenated fascism. They did not revolt against the Fascist regime as such, but rather against a system of government that no longer functioned in an orderly manner and against a leader who failed in wartime. Fascism had never been anything more than a means for the distribution of power. Now it had gotten out of control, had broken down under the strain of war, and had to be replaced. As in 1922, these same dominant interest groups sought a transition that would involve a minimum of risks. The conservatives also operated from a solid institutional base and had a unifying symbol in the king. This meant that conservative Italy would be relatively prepared for the postfascist political battles. During the crisis, the Fascist party simply dissolved without offering the slightest resistance. The fact that a three-million-member organization could vanish overnight reflected the emptiness of its ideology and political role. In short, all the "hyphenated" fascisms reverted back to their core beliefs and loyalties.

The failure of German and Italian arms led to the final government reorganization of the Fascist regime. Ciano, Grandi, and Bottai led the list of those who were replaced in February 1943. They were followed in April by Carmine Senise, who was dismissed as head of the political police, and by Aldo Vidussoni, who gave way to Carlo Scorza as secretary of the PNF. Scorza's appointment, a belated effort to recapture the old spirit of squadrism, brought to the leadership of the party the former ras of Lucca and one of the assassins of the great liberal Giovanni Amendola. Of course, none of these changes had the slightest effect, except to ensure that the ablest of the dismissed (Grandi, Bottai, Senise) would join the ranks of the plotters. The loss of the regime's control over the country became painfully apparent when a major, communist-led strike halted production in Turin and Milan in early March. Prominent industrialists, fearing the rise of a radical alternative, began to press for a separate understanding with the British and the Americans. Vittorio Cini, the minister of communications and representative of the Confindustria in the new government, offered his resignation after presenting the bleakest possible picture of Italian transport capabilities.

The center of the various conspiracies to remove Mussolini was Duke Pietro Acquarone, minister of the Royal Household, senator, and financier. Two parallel sets of conspiracies developed around Acquarone. Contacts were established with prefascist political leaders and with the chiefs of the various military and police forces. Another series of contacts were made with moderate Fascists, like Grandi, who sought to preserve some of the legacy of fascism by dumping Mussolini and installing a military government under Caviglia. After the fall of the island of Pantelleria in May, it became clear that the Allied invasion of Sicily could not be far off. By then, Hitler, whose relationship with Mussolini was based purely on sentiment, regarded Italian territory exclusively in terms of German occupation. The two men met twice during these months—in April at Klessheim, and in July at Feltre. The last meeting resulted in a total misunderstanding between Mussolini and his military and political advisers. General Ambrosio wanted the Duce to inform the Germans that Italy could not continue the war. Typically, Mussolini, rather than convey the bad news, allowed himself to be buoyed up by Hitler. The invasion of Sicily on July 9, coupled with the failure of the Feltre meeting to open a way out of the war, proved the final straw for those who felt that a change of leadership was essential. Even pro-Nazis, like Scorza and Farinacci, pressed for changes. They wanted Ambrosio out and the pro-German Marshall Rodolfo Graziani installed as leader of the armed forces. They also wanted to bind the monarchy closer to the Fascist war effort. To this end, they were willing to use a meeting of the Fascist Grand Council to pressure Mussolini. The anti-German group of Grandi, Bottai, and Federzoni also planned to use the Grand Council to offer a motion that would restore political initiative to the king, who would then replace Mussolini with either Caviglia or Badoglio. On July 15, Mussolini agreed to convene a meeting of the Grand Council for the first time since 1939.

The session, which began on July 24 and ended in the early hours of July 25, could not have come under more dramatic circumstances. The Allies were in Sicily and the Germans were watching events in Rome intently. No one had a clear idea what might happen after a vote against Mussolini. The Grand Council's powers were unclear on this point, and it is likely that Mussolini, certain of the king's support, was determined to ignore any vote. Dino Grandi arrived at the meeting with grenades hidden away in case Mussolini ordered the arrest of the conspirators. The leaders of the opposition had no way of estimating the effect on wavering members of the Grand Council of a determined counterattack by Mussolini.

This counterattack never came, however. After a weak defense of the alliance with Germany and the conduct of the war, Mussolini turned the floor over to his opponents. Grandi, Bottai, and Ciano all rose to denounce the German alliance and to call for a new direction in policy. During a pause, Grandi circulated among the members to gather signatures for his motion that called for resumption of power on the part of the king with no reference to continued fighting on the side of the Nazis. When the vote came, shortly after midnight on July 25, Grandi's motion carried nineteen to seven, with one abstention. Among the majority was Ciano, who, although he did not know it, had signed his death warrant.

Informed of the decision of the Grand Council, the royal palace mobilized the army and the police. When Mussolini, who was strangely passive throughout these hours, visited the king in the afternoon, he was told of his dismissal and replacement by Badoglio and immediately arrested. Faced with a fait accompli, the leaders of the PNF counseled their members to accept the royal action. Within a matter of hours the regime had crumbled. The new government under Marshall Badoglio imprisoned Mussolini on the island of Ponza and then atop the Gran Sasso mountain, from which the Germans rescued him on September 12. Meanwhile Badoglio attempted simultaneously to assure the Germans that nothing had changed and to negotiate an end of the war with the Anglo-Americans. Italy's withdrawal from the war came on September 8, 1943, and was followed almost immediately by the German occupation of Italy. Mussolini, from his German refuge, proclaimed the creation of a new Fascist republican state on September

15. The Fascist regime had fallen, only to rise again in a new form under German protection. Its legacy would be civil war and further defeat.

Chapter Nine
*The Italian Social
Republic
1943–45*

The Structure of the Republic

The Italian Social Republic, or the Republic of Salò (from the name of the town where the Foreign Ministry was located), raises several important issues for our understanding of Italian fascism. How should the return to republicanism and social populism be judged? Was it the real essence of fascism or just a last desperate gamble to establish a social and political base?

The Fascist republic represented only a partial break with past practices. Certainly the style of government did not change. The Social Republic duplicated on a smaller scale the system of fiefdoms which had marked the regime. But there were important differences. The conservative fellow travelers were missing from Salò. The new regime had no real support from the industrialists, the Church, or the cultural establishment. The political core of the republic was composed of three groups. There were the pro-Germans, whose option for the Axis and identification with an intransigent fascism precluded jumping to support of the monarchy and Badoglio. Roberto Farinacci, the ras of Cremona, departed for Germany almost immediately after the vote in the Grand Council. He was joined by the violent anti-Semite Giovanni Preziosi and former government ministers Alessandro Pavolini and Renato Ricci. These men vied for the mantle of succession. A second important group was made up of opportunists, like the longtime undersecretary at the Interior Ministry Guido Buffarini Guidi, whose ties to the German embassy in Rome left him only one direction in which to develop his taste for political intrigue. Along side the opportunists were those who joined out of professional jealousy, like Marshall Rodolfo Graziani, who could be counted on to oppose his rival Badoglio. Finally, there were a number of bureaucrats and officials who simply found themselves in the wrong place and opted for the path of least resistance. A third group was composed of Mussolinians, like Giorgio Pini, a relatively moderate Fascist journalist, who rallied more to the person of the Duce than to the regime. They were flanked by a few national syndicalists whose unending willingness to be deceived led them to hope that something might be accomplished under German protection.

Motivations for supporting the republic ranged from Giovanni Preziosi's dream of a final solution to the Jewish problem, to Buffarini Guidi's opportunism, to a confused radicalism or misplaced sense of national honor after the surrender to the Allies. If this shrunken social and political base of the Salò Republic was a notable difference from historic fascism, the omnipresent German occupation was the reality which totally conditioned the life of the new regime. Hitler's political and military advisers had been opposed to a rump Italian government. They preferred to allow purely military considerations to triumph. Faced with Hitler's adamant desire to see the Duce liberated and restored to power, the Germans were determined to limit as far as possible the consequences of the Führer's choice. Italy was divided into two areas by Germany. Northeastern Italy (Udine, Gorizia, Trieste, Fiume, and Pola, along with the Italian Tyrol) was placed under direct German administration and treated as de facto German territory. The rest of Italy was considered occupied territory. The effect was to limit substantially the Social Republic's administrative control of its own territory. In addition, the Germans established their own parallel administration to oversee the Italian government, and they were determined not to allow social and economic experimentation to interfere with war production.

The new state had no capital (neither the Germans nor Mussolini wanted the Duce to return to Rome), no army, no constitution, and no diplomatic recognition, except by direct satellites of Germany. Even Franco's Spain refused to establish formal diplomatic relations. The administrative apparatus was spread out like spilled marbles over northern Italy: the Foreign Office at Salò, Defense at Cremona, Corporations at Verona, Agriculture at Treviso, National Education at Padua, Justice at Brescia, the bureaucracies and records in Rome. All communications were in the hands of the Germans, so that even Mussolini, who resided in the village of Gargnano, could never exercise effective control over his own government.

To further complicate the existing problems, for almost two years, from the time of the armistice between the Badoglio government and the Allies and the subsequent occupation of Italy by the Germans after September 8, 1943, the country was the scene of a double battle. There was the major military conflict between the Anglo-Americans and the German forces, which led to a slow liberation of Italy from Naples northward. But there was also a parallel civil war that set the Royal government, established in Brindisi after the German occupation of Rome and expanded in April 1944 to include most of the democratic parties in the Council of National Liberation, against the military forces of Salò. The second struggle assumed major proportions in the North where the Resistance was able to field a sizeable army in 1944–45 against the militia of the Social Republic.

The Creation of the Italian Social Republic

The decision to set up a government emerged after the Germans rescued Mussolini from his prison on the Gran Sasso mountain on September 12, 1943. The Duce was brought to Germany, where he had meetings on September 14 and 15 with Hitler and a small group of Fascists who were in Germany. The new government reflected both the diminished possibilities and the depleted personnel of reborn fascism. The new party secretary was Alessandro Pavolini, who had undergone a startling transformation. Once a writer of short stories and editor of Florentine political-literary reviews, he became minister of popular culture and then secretary of the Republican Fascist party and dreamed of dying with his men in a bloody massacre. Perhaps Farinacci came closest to the truth when he described Pavolini as a fanatic who understood nothing whatsoever of politics. The head of the militia was the brutal former ras of Massa Carrara, Renato Ricci, who had rendered undistinguished service in a number of ministerial posts. Other positions were filled by second-level and marginal men: Ferdinando Mezzasoma as minister of popular culture; Piero Pisenti, a bureaucrat, as justice minister; Buffarini Guidi as interior minister; and Mussolini as foreign minister (because no Italian diplomat of stature would take the post). Referred to as the "Grand Duchy of Tuscany" (Buffarini, Ricci, and Pavolini were Tuscans), the new regime was torn by rivalries, divided in purpose, and paralyzed between different power centers. Alongside the army, at least four different private and semiofficial militias existed: the Republican National Guard under Ricci, special police under Buffarini, the Black Brigades under Pavolini, and various independent squads that were tied to important *ras* like Farinacci. A key initial battle was lost over the army. Graziani hoped to use the Italian prisoners in Germany as the nucleus of the Republican army and to win control over all military forces within the Republic. The Germans, however, refused to release more than a handful of the half-million prisoners, and the party forced Mussolini to grant its militia a special status.

The Congress of Verona: The Constitutional Underpinnings

The closest the Social Republic came to a formal constitution was the program produced by the first and only congress of the reconstituted Republican Fascist party, which was held in Verona in November 1943. The mood of this congress was intransigent and violent. The enemies of the Fascist Republicans were the moderates who voted against Mussolini on July 25. The party manifesto called for a republican government, elected on the basis of popular sovereignty. Catholicism was to remain the official religion, and Jews were to be treated as foreigners. Although there was some feeling in the party for internal democracy, old habits died hard. Elections were promised for lower offices, but the party secretary and the government would be appointed by the Duce.

Perhaps the most interesting parts of the Verona program were devoted to social and economic policy. The proposed system differed from the state-directed capitalism of the earlier regime. As might be expected, when the conservative restraints were removed, the Fascist syndicalists and populists, who were radical in their views, had freer rein for their dream of a "third way" between capitalism and socialism. Most private property was still guaranteed by the new regime, but social control, or socialization of production, became the goal. Nationalization of public services and war industries was promised. Uncultivated land or land that was not being used productively was to be divided among day laborers or handed to farmer cooperatives. Social control in industry would operate by means of state ownership of key sectors and the establishment of management councils and profit sharing in the private sector. These plans were given substance in a decree law of February 12, 1944. All firms with a capitalization of more than one million lire were to be socialized. a four-level management system was to be imposed, consisting of an assembly, composed of equal parts of workers and shareholders, a managerial council of capital and labor, a syndical college, and a director, who was elected by the assembly, or in the state sectors, chosen by the government. In cases of poor management, the directors of state firms could be removed by the minister of corporative economy, or in private firms by the administrative council. The government itself would draw up the overall plan within which each firm would operate.

In a reversal of earlier decision that placed the technocratic element with ownership, the Social Republic made a significant move to give technical and managerial personnel an independent role between capital and labor. In all cases, however, the shareholders still had a fairly strong voice. They constituted half the assembly in private corporations, and the usual hierarchies were respected despite the rhetoric about reducing the role of capital. The new system did not even mark a victory for Fascist syndicalism. The unions were not really in control of the managers, nor did they have a part in state planning.

The response to Fascist "social control" was almost universally negative. The Germans exempted almost the entire industrial system from the socialization provisions. The Fascists were divided. Interior Minister Buffarini was opposed to experimentation, and Farinacci realistically argued that all plans would have to wait until the end of the war. Perhaps the most dramatic response came from the workers, who began a massive strike on March 1, 1944. It was not just the desperate economic conditions that produced this worker protest. A large part of the northern factory proletariat had never abandoned its loyalties to the Socialist and Communist parties. The Fascist intermediate elites within the unions were never really able to create a positive allegiance in the northern cities. They had merely reduced their opponents to silence without converting them. During the brief period of political freedom in August 1943, the traditional left reappeared in the factories, while the Fascist labor organizations crumbled. When the Fascists returned to power as Nazi camp followers, the workers regarded the socialization projects as a sham. Thus, labor, which had been a problem for fascism earlier, remained so under the Social Republic despite a decree law of December 20, 1943, which established a single labor confederation in charge of all social and welfare agencies. As with many of the initiatives of the Social Republic, it is hard to say what might have happened over the long term. What did happen immediately was a second decree of April 3, 1944, which delayed the implementation of the single confederation and allowed the old, ineffective labor federations to operate as they had done in the past. The aspirations of the Fascist syndicalists for a union structure that would be independent of state and party control remained pure theory.

The response of the industrialists to the social innovations of Mussolini's new regime was even more negative than it had been under the earlier Fascist corporative system. The Social Republic had virtually no industrial backers, and the rare gestures of support for socialization were designed to sabotage the program. Faced with the appearance of total impotence, the Fascist government in July 1944 imposed the socialization laws on publishing firms, one of the few industries under its control. The results of the experiment might have been reassuring to the industrialists, if they had cared. At the *Corriere della Sera* of Milan, owned by the Crespi family, and at the Garzanti publishing house, the elections merely reconfirmed family control. When there was an effort to extend the system to Fiat in 1945, the Fascists failed even to organize an election.

The Collapse of the Social Republic

The leaders of the Social Republic sought legitimacy at the beginning of

1944 by trying in court those who had voted against Mussolini at the meeting of the Grand Council in July 1943. The Verona trials, held in January were designed as a condemnation of the Grand Council meeting and, in a broader sense, of the whole conservative legacy of earlier monarchical fascism. Unfortunately, all of the important leaders had escaped, with the exception of the old and feeble Emilio De Bono, and Galeazzo Ciano, who had not been closely connected with Grandi's conspiracy and who had unwisely entrusted his fate to the Germans, who hated him. The unlucky Ciano served the Fascist Republicans as the scapegoat for all the failures in their own past. The mediocre leaders who gathered under the banner of the Social Republic were determined to condemn him along with De Bono and a few others. The death sentence was a foregone conclusion (although Ciano hoped to the last that he might save himself by trading his diaries for his life). It was a fitting symbol of the Fascist Republic that the firing squad botched the execution and had to butcher the survivors individually.

The steady retreat of the German armies inevitably meant that the area under the control of the Social Republic diminished as the proximity of the front increased. The Germans simply absorbed the territory of the Republic into the area of military operations. Rome was liberated in June 1944 and large parts of central Italy soon followed. The year ended with the Duce pleading with the Germans to allow him to establish his capital in Milan. The Republic became more of a phantom government with each passing day, and it is doubtful that anyone except the Germans really controlled the political system. Certainly Mussolini lacked the will and the power to do so. Not only were the ministries out of his control, but so were the military and various police forces. The most obvious sign of his political eclipse was his loss of control over the Interior Ministry, a post which he had held uninterruptedly from 1926 to 1943 but which he surrendered to Buffarini during the Social Republic. Only in February 1945 did Mussolini summon the will to defy the Germans by dismissing Buffarini. By then, however, what Mussolini did made little difference to the Germans. In March and April the Nazis carried on secret negotiations with the Allies for surrender, while the Duce ineffectually sought to establish contact with the British through the Catholic Church. The last days of the regime were a minor chapter in the general collapse of German power. On April 25, 1945, Mussolini fled Milan, a day before the city fell into the hands of the Resistance forces. His escape to Como lasted only a day. On April 27, he joined a German convoy fleeing northward. When the trucks were stopped by a roadblock, set up by the Resistance, Mussolini was discovered cowering in a German uniform in the back of one of the vehicles. On April 28 he was executed, and the next day his body was exposed alongside that of his mistress, Clara Petacci, in the Piazzale Loreto in Milan, where, almost a year earlier, the Fascist squads had perpetrated one of their most vicious reprisals against the Resistance. The useless and bloody coda to the Fascist era passed into history.

Chapter Ten
*The Political Culture
of Fascism:
Ideologies and
Intellectuals*

Fascist ideology, like the regime of hyphenated fascisms itself, is not one but several realities. What one discovers depends in large part on where one looks. It is quite possible to cite Fascist pronouncements that seem revolutionary, others that are extremely conservative. Therefore, sweeping pronouncements by the Fascists themselves about the nature of their movement and their accomplishments in reshaping Italy must be taken seriously but also cautiously. The preceding chapters point to the inescapable conclusion that any connection between the way the regime actually functioned and official justifications was purely coincidental. For instance, corporative theory differed so radically from economic practice as to create an Alice-in-Wonderland effect.

The appeal of fascism in Italy was often independent of the political and economic policies of the regime. The explanation, put forward by militant antifascism of both liberal and socialist varieties, that a decent Italy had been occupied by a band of alien or capitalist oppressors is quite misleading. Fascism was not entirely divorced from a *healthy* Italian tradition or imposed on an unwilling country, which awaited the moment to throw off the yoke of oppression and resume the interrupted course of democracy. In fact, fascism managed to develop a broad, if only passive, consensus after the elimination of any real alternative in 1925 and the integration of Catholics into the regime after 1929. Some elements of the Fascist appeal—nationalism, the cult of the Duce, the image of a tough and respected Italy on the world stage, the call for social justice implied in corporativism—evoked a positive response from Italians until the late 1930s when the government's conduct of both foreign and domestic policy undermined the sense of inevitability which the regime had created around itself. Three things must be kept in mind about the consensus that Mussolini managed to create between 1929 and 1936. First, by the late 1920s the Fascists had all but eliminated any alternatives or rivals. (Residual loyalties to socialism and communism in centers such as Bologna, Turin, and Milan certainly remained strong because people rapidly reverted back to these older loyalties after 1942.) The generation that came of age in the late 1920s and 1930s had no reason to believe that Mussolini's regime would not last. Second, as we shall see, the Fascist state went to great lengths to coopt all but overt opponents in various initiatives sponsored by the regime. Finally, much of the fragile and untested consensus revolved around Mussolini personally. Throughout the 1930s the Duce remained far more popular than his Fascist party.

Fascism's strength derived from its nature as a composite movement which appealed to different constituencies without ever settling on a single fully accepted official definition. In the preceding chapters we have shown how fascism developed as several separate movements allied for civil war against the Socialist-led workers and peasants. The alliance followed the classic pattern by reducing the common program to a few points. By 1922 there were six parts to the Fascist coalition, each one with its own program and purpose.

National Syndicalism and Populism

National syndicalism was the original nucleus of the Fascist ideology. It evolved out of the classical syndicalist position that the workers' syndical or union organizations, not the Socialist political party, might be the basis for proletarian revolutionary action. The national syndicalists held that Italy could be organized as a society of producers, which would include both manual workers and managerial and technical personnel in each branch of industry. The mixed syndicate would be the basis for a new national political and economic order. The national syndicalist ideology was republican, anticlerical, and vaguely socialistic in the sense that its adherents did not view with favor capitalism without some direct worker participation in management. Although Mussolini had never been a syndicalist, many of his close associates had been involved in socialist and syndicalist politics, and most of them, including Mussolini, had been caught up in the revision of classical Marxism that had taken place under the impact of new theories on the functions of elite groups and political myths in controlling and moving masses. Gaetano Mosca, Gustave Le Bon, Vilfredo Pareto, and Georges Sorel all contributed to the intellectual milieu out of which national syndicalism emerged by shaking confidence in the Marxist revolutionary vision of the emancipation of the proletariat through the economic evolution of modern capitalism.

Mussolini and his friends simply lost faith that Italy had evolved to the point where a Marxist-style revolution was possible. Their activism led them to seek other alternatives. Both the Libyan war of 1911 and, more clearly, World War I were seen as a chance for the proletariat to rejoin the national community and accelerate the process of change toward a new society in which productive labor would have a leading role. The national syndicalists' decision to put their political aspirations in a purely national framework marked a decisive break with the internationalist ideals of Italian socialism and caused them to lose their working-class following. This was particularly true in the case of Mussolini, who went from being one of the most popular figures within the Socialist party to a virtual outcast. Mussolini's revolutionary purpose was gone; what remained was a hatred of the status quo and a predisposition to violent change. During the war the future Duce and his band of dissident socialists and syndicalists openly called for a union of all producers, regardless of class, in the name of victory against an enemy that included, in addition to the Austrians and Germans, the antiwar Socialists and Giolittians.

The first program of the Fascist movement in March 1919 was an expression of the desire of these former socialists and syndicalists to combine some residual socialism with extreme nationalism. Their perspective was that of the wartime coalitions of leftist parties that favored Italian participation in the conflict. This 1919 program called for lowering the voting age to eighteen, abolishing the existing monarchical constitution, and convening a constitutional assembly to draw up a new set of institutions for the country. In economic policy these national syndicalists demanded confiscation of excess war profits, an eight-hour day, and an increase in the minimum wage. Foreign policy was not dealt with in great detail, but Mussolini's participation in the violent demonstrations in favor of Italian territorial demands in Dalmatia and Fiume left no doubt about his position. In fact, despite the leftist rhetoric, nationalism figured as the framework for all political action. The political target of the Fascist movement was not the capitalist or landowner, rather it was the vaguely defined war profiteer and the Catholic, liberal, and socialist politicians who had opposed the war. The 1919 program appealed to veterans and discontented students but won few middle-class converts and offered nothing to the established social and economic elites.

Hopes for a syndical reorganization of the Italian economy continued to be held by intellectuals, such as Sergio Panunzio, and by leaders of the Fascist union movement, such as Edmondo Rossoni, whose journal *La Stirpe* argued that labor organizations had to be an independent power base against management, the party, and the corporative bureaucracy. But Rossoni's bid to make the unions into the major force in the political system under fascism was thwarted by the break up of the union confederation in 1928.

Antidemocratic Modernism

Recently, the historian Walter Adamson described a number of young intellectuals in the years just before World War I as modernist rebels who forged an adversary culture that broke with the positivist, democratic, optimistic, and materialist outlook of the nineteenth century (Walter L. Adamson, *Avant-Garde Florence: From Modernism to Fascism* [Cambridge: Harvard University Press,

1993]). Futurists such as Filippo Tommaso Marinetti rejected the nineteenth-century dogma that modern industrial progress would lead to political democracy and equality. They were joined by cultural rebels and avowed antidemocratic elitists, including Giuseppe Prezzolini and Giovanni Papini, who argued in *Lacerba*, *La Voce*, and other reviews that cultural rebirth for Italy could only come through an idealist or spiritual renewal. The cultural critique of these intellectuals and artists contributed to the development of fascism and of Mussolini's outlook in two ways. First, the Futurists conceived of politics as aesthetics, a vision unfettered by economic and social realities that would be the prerogative of a new elite or aristocracy of the spirit. Their modern world was governed by instinct, violence, and irrational forces expressed in terms of modern myths that were far from the optimistic, pacifist, and rationalist faith of democratic progressives. As Mussolini moved from the idea of a proletarian revolution to violent change as an end in itself, he came very close to the psychology of the Futurists and other aesthetic rebels for whom any status quo was insufferable. Second, the modernist vision of a spiritual aristocracy doing battle against materialism, egalitarian, and democratic mediocrity fed a search for heroes who could reverse the slide into degeneration and decadence. Neither fascism nor nazism would have been as attractive to interwar intellectuals without the pre-existing cult of the hero. In 1919 the Futurists enrolled under Mussolini's banner and his program of direct action and generic rebellion.

Squadrismo: Ruralist Fascism

Closely connected to the original nucleus of fascism was a mentality which might be best called *squadrismo*. It was the romantic vision of veterans, provincial students, and small-town professionals and businessmen who flocked to fascism in 1920 and 1921 in order to fight the "reds." Squadrismo was an anarchic explosion of violence that contained antiurban, antimodern, and antiindustrial elements. The young Black Shirts who embarked in their trucks to purge the countryside of subversives were imbued with a quasi-religious faith and a sense of heroism and sacrifice, as they relived the experience of the Great War against fellow Italians in the Po Valley. Later, its literary representatives, Curzio Malaparte and Mino Maccari, boisterously attacked both the upper-middle-class, cosmopolitan elite groups of the big cities and the antinational socialists.

Provincial squadrism claimed to represent the true Italy of the peasant soldiers. It reflected the authentic desire of the provincial lower middle class to become the spokesmen of rural Italy and thereby emerge as the new political class, but the fate of the movement hinged on the outcome of the political struggle of the ras to maintain their independence. This cause received an immediate setback when able and ambitious provincials, such as Dino Grandi in Bologna and Italo Balbo in Ferrara, opted for compromise with Mussolini and a career in national politics. The cause was definitively lost in 1925 when Mussolini chose the state bureaucracy rather than the party as the instrument of authoritarian dictatorship. Both politically and emotionally, squadrismo was at odds with Mussolini's compromise with the conservative establishment; its ideology never became more than a noisy polemic against cosmopolitanism. However, once the anarchic, violent spontaneity of original squadrismo was tamed, the Fascists created a mythology about the years of struggle and a cult of the fallen in a vain effort to inspire a younger generation. During the late 1930s the movement had a brief revival when it merged with the antimodernism and anti-Semitism of extreme pro-Nazi fascism. Farinacci, the last of the old-time ras, even created the Cremona Prize to reward those artists whose creativity took the form of the primitive peasant scenes, bucolic landscapes, and muscular male nudes that were in vogue in Nazi Germany.

Technocratic Fascism

A fourth element within the general Fascist consensus was technocratic fascism. This too was an expression of the desire of the

Italian middle class, but it differed sharply from squadrismo over ends and means. The origins of this movement can be found in the "competence groups" which were formed in 1921 to prepare the party for the technical task of governing. The Fascist veterans' movement also reflected the desires of returning officers for a larger role in postwar politics. Their slogan was "make way for abilities." The spokesman for technocratic fascism was Giuseppe Bottai, who gathered young intellectuals around his reviews, *Critica Fascista* and the *Archivio di Studi Corporativi*. Technocratic fascism was elitist and urban. Its aim was controlled modernization which accepted industrialization and sought to master the resulting problems of mass society through corporative organization and planning. The Fascist technocrats hoped to use a highly selective party as the basis for a new political and economic elite that would operate within the state, corporative, and syndical bureaucracies.

Technocratic fascism had an enduring popularity with the young, who looked to Bottai as the leader most responsive to their demands for real change. Unfortunately, the technocrats ran up against determined resistance from industry to their projects for a true corporative system of planning under the direction of an independent state bureaucracy. Moreover, Bottai had earlier helped destroy the power of Rossoni's union movement so that no help could be expected from that source. In so far as technocratic fascism put forward autonomous demands of the urban middle-class intermediate elite groups, it had to be channeled into visible but harmless endeavors. During the 1930s its leading adherents were absorbed into the massive corporative and syndical bureaucracies without achieving any appreciable power. Bottai and his friends, however, continued to act as a bridge to a younger generation that grew up under fascism and wavered between a desire to give life to its institutions and opposition to the regime.

Populist, squadrist, and technocratic fascism were different voices of the lower middle class that rallied to fascism. Apart from the desire to replace the old political class, they shared little common ground in their practical programs. Each demanded a more extensive challenge to the existing order than Mussolini was prepared to tolerate. As a result, proponents of two other theories of what fascism meant were much more influential.

Conservative Fascism

Conservative fascism was perhaps the least ideological element in the Fascist coalition, but it was extremely important in shaping the outlook of the regime. This was the heart of the various hyphenated fascisms: industrial, agrarian, monarchist, Catholic. Most conservatives wanted to give little or no intellectual content to fascism *per se* but rather to absorb it within the traditional culture and the ideal of strong government. Their influence was felt in the 1921 program of the new Fascist party, which abandoned populist, republican, and anticlerical rhetoric in favor of a free-enterprise fascism that was compatible with both the Church and the monarchy.

Nationalist Fascism

The most coherent version of conservative fascism came from Italian nationalism. When the Italian Nationalist Association adhered to the Fascist party in March 1923 it brought three central ideas to the emerging Fascist consensus: the need to reinforce the state apparatus by removing constraints on executive power, the determination to control the mass proletarian organizations by incorporating them within the structure of the state, and the need for a strong foreign policy as a way of focusing national will. The Nationalists were at one with the less ideological conservatives in their defense of the monarchy and church, but they went further in their call for a reordering of the political system to cope with the development of mass politics. Two former leaders of the Nationalist Association played key roles in the construction of the Fascist state after 1922. Luigi Federzoni acted as interior minister from 1924 to 1926, just as the system of repression was created, and Alfredo Rocco as justice minister from 1925 to 1932 gave the

Fascist *state*, rather than the *party*, its legal and institutional framework. The Nationalists continued to hold prominent positions in
the foreign policy establishment and were extremely influential
in setting cultural policy. An ex-Nationalist, Antonio Maraini,
headed the Venice Biennale; another, Cipriano Effisio Oppo, dominated the Rome Quadriennale; and Dino Alfieri was one of the
creators of the enormously successful Exhibition of the Fascist
Revolution in 1932 and a future minister of popular culture in
1936.

The Common Denominator

The various parts of the Fascist coalition were united in their hatred of socialism; in their rejection of individualist, agnostic, and
pluralistic liberal values; and in their desire to overcome social
and economic fragmentation through an authoritarian state. All
Fascists came together on four points. *Nationalism* was the most
fundamental. The core of fascism was little more than extreme
nationalism—the cult of the state and nation. The historic mission of fascism was to complete national unity and achieve national greatness; the national framework was the standard for all
social and economic experiments and initiatives. In practice, this
was a triumph for the position of the Italian Nationalist Association, but it was also the expression of the views of the idealist
philosopher Giovanni Gentile that the ethical state was the source
of all that was truly human. Each individual could only realize
full intellectual and spiritual potential in so far as he or she participated in the formation of that national consciousness. From
both the Nationalist and Gentilean perspectives the individual was
subordinate to the state, whose strength was proportionate to the
single will which guided it. *Elitism* was a second common element. None of the Fascist ideological traditions believed in egalitarian democracy or pure majority rule. *Authoritarianism* was also
a common thread. Fascists of various persuasions accepted the
single party and the abolition of parliamentary democracy. External events, such as the Great Depression and the crises leading to

World War II, only reinforced the Fascist predilection toward stat-ist and authoritarian solutions. Nationalism, statism, and authoritarianism culminated in the cult of the Duce. Finally, *col-lectivism* was also important. The Fascists were aware that their movement had to reorganize a politicized mass society. Most were willing to experiment with new techniques of mass psychology and economic and political control in order to achieve their aims.

Despite general agreement on these four themes, it was hard to formulate a definition of fascism because of the fundamental dif-ferences over the nature of the movement. The conservatives and Nationalists tended to see fascism as a rejection of the ideological heritage of the French Revolution, but syndicalists and many tech-nocrats argued that fascism was a more modern, "social" devel-opment of the democratic revolutionary heritage and a corrective to the excessive individualism of liberal democracy. Gentile at-tempted to identify fascism with his actualist and idealist phi-losophy but provoked an outraged reaction from Catholics, who rejected the idea that the state could be the source of spiritual and moral values. Thus, it was not that fascism lacked an intellectual dimension, in fact, each of the components had its own tradition, which went deep into Italian intellectual life. As long as the re-gime demanded an essentially passive response, fascism benefited from the ability of each person to define the ideology in his or her own way. When the Fascists demanded an active response during the crises leading to World War II, cracks emerged in the consen-sus.

The Evolution of Fascist Political Culture during the Twenties

Until the Matteotti murder in 1924 sharpened the line between Fascists and their opponents and made outright dictatorship in-evitable, little could be done to formulate a coherent cultural policy. Distinctions were further blurred by friendships that had not been completely ruptured. The militant Fascist Curzio Malaparte could still frequent the young liberal editor Piero Gobetti, who would soon become a martyr to Fascist violence; others like journalist and cultural entrepreneur Giuseppe Prezzolini kept a foot in both camps. Only between 1925 and 1929, as the regime repressed vocal opposition, did it begin to organize its propaganda and cultural apparatus. In 1925 the Fascist Institute of Culture was created to bring the regime's message to the masses by means of libraries and lectures. A "Manifesto of Fascist Intellectuals," written by Giovanni Gentile and published at the end of the founding congress of the Fascist Institute of Culture, asserted that fascism was a vindication of the rights of the nation and of the state against the excesses of democracy and individualism. Fascism was a new *social* liberalism that aimed at the creation of a higher national consciousness than had been achieved by the liberal parliamentary state. The declaration was signed by a number of prominent intellectuals (not all Fascists), who responded to this generic conservative and nationalist appeal.

Despite its vagueness, the Fascist "Manifesto" provoked a counter-document from the pen of Italy's other leading philosopher, the liberal Benedetto Croce, who defended the traditional rights of free intellectual inquiry and autonomy from state direction. Croce's counter-manifesto was signed by most of Italy's best-known cultural figures. Faced with this sort of opposition from the cultural establishment, the regime rejected the option of a massive purge of the universities and the forcible imposition of its will on the intellectual community. Instead, it took the long-term approach of creating a new framework that would win over the majority of intellectuals by destroying all political alternatives.

In 1926, after the commotion over the various manifestos had died down, the government announced the creation of the Royal Academy of Italy, which was to be a first step to coopt the better-known intellectuals by honors and special privileges. At the same time, the Fascists moved to control the scores of local and provincial academies and institutes. Many merely added the term "fascist" to the letterhead, but during the 1930s special oaths of loyalty to the regime were also imposed on members of cultural organizations. Another small beginning was made during the twenties to introduce the corporative system into the arts and professions. In 1928 the National Confederation of Fascist Professional and Artistic Syndicates brought together various associations of architects, composers, painters, sculptors, musicians, and theatrical performers. Membership in a recognized professional association was made a prerequisite to enter a growing number of state-sponsored artistic competitions, such as the Venice Biennale or the Rome Quadriennale, or to submit designs for public works projects. As the historian Marla Stone has noted, the state, the Fascist party, and the leading political figures also became large scale purchasers of art for public and private collections (Marla Susan Stone, *The Patron State: Culture and Politics in Fascist Italy* [Princeton: Princeton University Press, 1998], pp. 70–79).

Organizations like the Royal Academy of Italy involved intellectuals publicly with the regime, but these institutions also entangled more radical and totalitarian-minded Fascists in traditional culture and made it more difficult to formulate a clear alternative to pre-Fascist conservatism. One need only to look at the names of presidents of the Royal Academy to see the problems faced by the regime in trying to disentangle itself from the past: the conservative Catholic ex-foreign minister Tommaso Tittoni, the inventor-industrialist Guglielmo Marconi, Gabriele D'Annunzio, the conservative Nationalist Luigi Federzoni, and Giovanni Gentile. In the end, the regime's collaboration with traditional culture enhanced the passive consensus that grew up around fascism during the early thirties, but it also reinforced the status quo against any effort by Fascist extremists to push toward a radical break with the past.

After 1926 intellectuals conformed to the external constraints imposed by the regime. Overt antifascism disappeared. Its leading exponents were in exile or in prison. But the largest number of less vocal opponents did not seek refuge abroad. Instead, they withdrew from active public life, while continuing to publish in their areas of expertise. Some liberal intellectuals rallied behind Benedetto Croce's journal, *La Critica*, which continued to defend the prefascist liberal state and liberal ideas. At the other extreme were the enthusiastic Fascists. The most notable conquests were Gentile, the historian Gioacchino Volpe, and, more ambiguously, Luigi Pirandello. In the middle was the mass of artists and intellectuals who accepted the regime and its commissions out of self-interest, because they saw no alternative or because they identified with one or more of the themes of generic nationalism without having to subscribe to an official doctrine.

During the late twenties hard-line Fascists like Roberto Forges-Davanzati argued that the government should attack the problem of the mobilization of apolitical intellectuals and suppression of quiet opponents by a complete purge of the universities. These Fascist cultural extremists correctly understood that the failure to dominate the cultural establishment meant that the regime's hold on the political and economic system would never be entirely secure. Such appeals, however, went unheeded. Mussolini's cultural policies paralleled his method of rule in politics and precluded clear and decisive action. The Fascist regime continued to respect the boundaries of traditional culture and to refuse to define its own alternative except in generic terms.

Early Fascist Educational Reform

An example of the Fascist regime's inability to escape the domination of Italy's traditional culture can be seen in its approach to the problem of education. On taking power, the Fascist movement had no fixed ideas on educational policy, yet, ironically, the first major piece of legislation, defined by Mussolini as the "most Fascist reform," dealt with education. The man responsible for this curious situation was Gentile, appointed minister of public instruction in the first government. The Gentile reform of 1923 was the work of conservative elitists and philosophical idealists who had been crusading for changes in the schools long before fascism began its march to power. They were determined to use the opportunity provided by authoritarian government to ensure that the schools would become the means by which the young might approach the realm of the spirit through real communication between teacher and student. Obviously, such an aim involved only the best students and centered on the university-oriented humanistic curriculum with philosophy as its unifying discipline.

Gentile's reform concentrated on the pre-university high schools, the classical *ginnasio-liceo* program, which emphasized philosophy, Latin, and history. Even in the newly created scientific high schools a strong emphasis on the humanities existed, and in teacher-training institutes, established on the high school and university levels, child psychology and modern pedagogy were subordinated to philosophy.

Gentile hoped that by rigidly separating technical and professional education from the classical program and by severely restricting those who might enter the classical program, education would be returned to its true purpose of elite formation. To this end, Gentile created a series of extremely rigorous state examinations which the students had to pass upon completion of the *liceo* and before entering the university. On the whole, the new legislation was motivated by the ideal that the student-professor relationship was sacrosanct. Although the authority of the rectors and headmasters was strengthened, a degree of academic freedom and the autonomy of the university over its own affairs survived.

Not unexpectedly, the Gentile reform was far too elitist to satisfy the aspirations of fascism's middle-class constituencies. The government was immediately deluged with complaints from parents about the difficult state examination. Similarly, the Catholic Church, which gained mandatory religious instruction in elementary schools and official recognition of the Catholic University of Milan, disliked Gentile's refusal to introduce Catholic dogma in the upper-level schools. Finally, the reform displeased the Fascist extremists because it failed to provide a mechanism whereby the universities could be purged of those hostile to the regime and because it offered no instrument to wage the cultural battle within the intellectual elite. Thus, Gentile's reform suffered the fate of any comprehensive and coherent plan in a regime of hyphenated fascisms. As soon as Gentile left the government in June 1924, his reform was subjected to piecemeal dismantling under a dizzying succession of education ministers. Rules governing the difficult state examinations were eased and religious instruction was extended in a gesture to win Catholic support. As a result, enrollments, after bottoming out in the late twenties, began to increase rapidly after 1930. Between 1931 and 1939 the number of students in the *ginnasio-liceo* doubled and tripled in teacher-training institutes. By 1933 university enrollment returned to 1922 levels and rose rapidly thereafter. Pressure on professional and white-collar employment continued to be intense and left the regime without a plan to satisfy the very constituency, which it needed to placate.

Almost by necessity, then, the Fascist regime was forced to take the long view in its effort to shape Italy's young. Rather than attack the schools directly, parallel organizations were established, such as the *Opera Nazionale Balilla* (ONB) in 1926 and the *Fascio Giovanile del Littorio* in 1930. A separate organization for university students, the *Gruppi Universitari Fascisti* (GUF), operated under the direct control of the secretary of the PNF. Coordination between Fascist youth organizations and the elementary schools was extensive. Rural schools were put under the control of the ONB, teachers served as instructors in the Balilla, and the schools offered time for pupils to participate in Fascist youth activities. Integration was less successful on the university level where prefascist liberal culture was stronger. A feeble attempt to drive opponents from the university faculties by means of an oath of allegiance to the regime failed when only eleven professors refused to take it. This highly suspect unanimity provoked one Fascist official to mutter that the Jesuits had taught the Italians only too well the theory of "mental reservation."

Cultural Policies in the Thirties:
The Influence of Gentile

The major cultural initiative during the late twenties and early thirties was the publication of the *Italian Encyclopedia* under the direction of Gentile. The effort mobilized intellectuals of all political persuasions behind an official project of the regime, and Gentile ensured that no overt political standard would be applied to the scholarship. Except in the case of contributions that touched directly upon the interests of the regime, the articles reflected diverse points of view and were of high quality.

The entry on fascism, written by Gentile and Mussolini, was the closest the regime ever came to self-definition. Mussolini's contribution was practical and historical, but Gentile argued that fascism was a moral and ethical system that sought to elevate national consciousness. It was the political equivalent of Gentile's own philosophy, in which each individual thought and acted as part of the larger community. Constructive freedom demanded awareness of the needs and purposes of the collectivity. The mission of the Fascist state was to establish such spiritual harmonization between the individual and the collective will.

The ideas expressed in the entry on fascism never won wide acceptance. On a purely practical level, Gentile ran into the opposition of the Catholic Church, which rejected the ethical role given the state. The generation which came of age during the 1930s felt that despite Gentile's defense of the collectivity, his ideas lacked social and economic concreteness which they found in corporativism and, later, in communism. Finally, the very elitism of the theory bothered the Fascist extremists who believed, as Gentile did not, that consent had to be coerced from intellectuals.

Mass Propaganda and the Myth of the Duce

On the level of mass propaganda, the myth of the Duce increasingly became the core of the ideology as the regime moved toward simplified and ritualized thought and behavior. In 1933 Achille Starace, the sycophantic secretary of the Fascist party, decreed that the term *Duce* always had to be written in capital letters. Mussolini in heroic poses filled newsreels and office walls, and the slogan "the Duce is always right" tended to substitute for reasoned dialogue. Of course, the fawning Starace did not act on his own. Mussolini became convinced of his own destiny. Against the fears of advisers, he had managed the Ethiopian adventure without serious consequences. To those who warned that Italy's economic system would not support a major war, Mussolini countered with his own political sense of what was possible in any given situation.

The impact of war and the example of the Nazi propaganda machine under Josef Goebbels led the regime to experiment in new areas of social and political control. In 1933 Mussolini appointed his son-in-law Galeazzo Ciano to be head of the Press Office, which was still a division under the head of government. Ciano, who had studied the German example, immediately began to expand the role of the Press Office into radio and film. In September 1934 a subcabinet department, the Secretariat for Press and Propaganda, was created with specific competence for all media. That same month the General Directorate for Cinema was formed under Luigi Freddi, a journalist and ex-official in the Fascist youth movement. Similar offices for tourism and theater followed, and an oversight committee for radio was established. In June 1935 Ciano and Mussolini created a new Ministry of Press and Propaganda to direct this nascent bureaucracy. Finally, in May 1937, the propaganda machine was renamed the Ministry of Popular Culture or Minculpop. By then, Ciano had moved on to the Foreign Ministry; first Dino Alfieri, then Alessandro Pavolini was put in charge of the effort to bring Italian propaganda to the imperial level.

Italy never effectively centralized its cultural bureaucracy, however. The greatest success of the propaganda machine came during the Ethiopian war in 1935 and 1936, when existing enthusiasm was whipped into an active willingness to sacrifice for the national cause. Thereafter propaganda fell sort of expectations. Mussolini failed to appreciate fully the potential of radio; as a result, it was only occasionally used effectively. The cost of radio receivers remained high despite the best efforts of the regime to lower it. By 1939, in contrast to Germany, which had 9.5 million subscribers to radio, Italy had barely over 1 million and these were found in northern and central regions. The regime had only slightly more luck with film. Throughout the twenties and thirties American films took a large share of the Italian market until the Alfieri law of 1938 banned the distribution of foreign films. Overtly propagandistic Italian films never matched the popularity of films made for pure entertainment, but the government was able to use the vehicle of the newsreel more directly. Through the Istituto

LUCE (L'Unione per la Cinematografia Educativa) it produced newsreels and educational films which were distributed in commercial theaters and through the cinema network of the leisure-time Dopolavoro organization.

During the late thirties the problem was often not the inadequacy of the technical means but rather the quality of the message. Many of the propaganda targets, designed to penetrate the sphere of private life and behavior, were the subject of ridicule. The use of Christmas trees was discouraged as a foreign custom, as was the pronoun *lei* instead of *voi* for the formal *you* (which resulted in puns like "Galileo Galivoi"). There was a serious attempt to mimic the French Jacobin revolutionaries of 1793 by shifting the celebration of the New Year to October 28, and the calendar was changed to reflect the years of the Fascist era.

The School Charter of 1939

The final serious effort to create a new Fascist political man came with the School Charter of 1939. In fact, the charter was the last major domestic initiative of any sort and resulted from a decade-long preoccupation with the failure to break down the traditional system of education and elite formation (which had been reinforced by the Gentile reform). The Fascist School Charter, drafted under the direction of Giuseppe Bottai, minister of national education from 1936 to 1943, envisaged an educational system that would conform more closely to the ruralist and populist rhetoric of fascism. In short, a new Fascist man was finally to emerge as the product of the regime. As usual, the results were far more influenced by traditional values than official statements would have one believe. Special schools were established for the children of peasants and craftsmen in order to increase their attachment to the land and to reinforce rural hierarchies. The reform sought to ease unemployment in the professions by shifting students out of programs leading to the universities and into technical training programs which did not lead to higher degrees. A step was made to democratize the schools by extending the age of common schooling, but the point at which children were tested and tracked into specialized schools was set at eleven years, too low to overcome the disadvantages of poorer family backgrounds. Bottai left the classical high-school program, which had been the core of traditional middle-class culture, largely as Gentile designed it, but rules governing the difficult state examination were eased. One of the innovations of the reform was the introduction of manual labor as an educational tool on all levels of schooling. The idea was an attempt to fuse modern theories of education, such as the encouragement of creativity and curiosity on the part of the pupil, with the populist tradition in fascism that no one was exempt from labor in a nation of producers. The failure to fund the program in wartime and resistance from middle-class families aborted the scheme.

The School Charter represented an elaborate effort to reconcile controlled social change with the need for a modern labor force. It is difficult to say how far the Fascist government might have gone in trying to shape the student population, but the initial results did not indicate that the break with past policy was sharp enough to create a distinctive Fascist educational system.

The Fascist University Generation and the Problem of a New Political Class

There were many attempts to mobilize the university generation outside the classroom. One of the more interesting efforts was the institution of the *Littoriali* for Art and Culture in 1934 as a national university competition in the social sciences, fine arts, and humanities. Contests were first held in smaller towns and university centers and, finally, on the national level. The themes were selected by the government with the aim of raising political and ideological consciousness among students. In fact, political consciousness was often raised but not in ways intended by the regime. One of the curious features of the Fascist system was that it allowed greater freedom to the student and youth press to discuss issues. Students used the occasion of the national competition to raise questions that penetrated dangerously far behind the facade projected by the regime. Reports circulated that several of the leading contestants in 1938 were arrested for subversive activities, and it is certain that the *Littoriali* produced many future Catholic, socialist, and communist leaders, as well as postfascism's most prominent writers and film directors. By the eve of World War II many young people were but a step away from overt antifascism.

Art, Architecture, and Race

By the late 1930s the leading Fascists were aware that the failure to hammer out a single policy on culture and a coherent ideology meant that the linkage between the political class and the mass base, which should have been provided by a solidly formed class of Fascist intellectuals and intermediate elites, was extremely weak. The result was that large sections of the masses were escaping from participation in the regime, but there was no agreement on how best to remedy the situation. On the one hand, the Ministry of Popular Culture acted to increase direct control over intellectual life. An expression of this drive came during the racial campaign, which was directed not only against the Jews but also at modern "Jewish" culture. In 1938 a committee was formed to purge literature of decadent (avant-garde) and Jewish authors. Roberto Farinacci, whose interest in art normally was limited to attractive female opera singers but who could seize an opportunity when it was presented, jumped on the bandwagon by creating the Cremona Prize to reward art that glorified Fascist values of nation and race.

Yet, just when a combination of Fascist intransigents, anti-Semites, and cultural conservatives geared up to declare war on modern art and culture, Mussolini allowed his veteran minister of National Education, Bottai, to create a rival power center to the Ministry of Popular Culture in the educational bureaucracy. Bottai, the most culturally open of all Fascist leaders, realized that a plunge into blind reaction would only have increased the alienation between intellectuals and the regime.

Three cultural constituencies would have resisted rigid controls. The largest bloc was composed of apolitical artists who wished to continue working without government interference. Because there had never been an official policy on art, no massive flight of creative talent had taken place. (Arturo Toscanini's decision not to conduct in Italy after having been roughed up for refusing to play the Fascist anthem before a concert in Bologna was an exception.) The coexistence of the visual arts, an area in which Italy excelled during the early twentieth century, and fascism was especially notable. Important painters like Giorgio Morandi, Giorgio De Chirico, Carlo Carrà, Filipo De Pisis, and Felice Casorati worked within the country.

Two movements which developed between the end of World War I and 1925 reflected a conservative artistic outlook and a renewal of classical values: *Valori Plastici* (1918–21) and *Novecento* (1923–circa 1931). In both these expressions a deliberate return to order, form, and balance, if not to traditional canons of realism predominated. Yet *Novecento*, which had the formidable backing of Margherita Sarfatti, Mussolini's mistress, cultural mentor, and editor of the party review *Gerarchia*, never became the official school of the regime, nor was there any uniformity in the interpretation of realism and tradition, which spanned from De Chirico's use of precise forms in a metaphysical context to the perfect and tranquil still-lifes of Giorgio Morandi. Another group which vied for recognition as *the* Fascist art form was Futurism. Despite Marinetti's prominence in the regime and his ability to advance the interests of the artists associated with his movement, he was never able to convince Mussolini to make futurism the official Fascist art. Marinetti, however, did remain as a determined proponent of cultural openness and modernity against the encroachments of the Nazi-inspired intransigents. Thus, despite all the calls for a return to conservative traditions, there was even a lively group of abstract artists like Carlo Radice, Manlio Rho, and Gino Ghiringhelli who opted for geometrical forms which had much in common with Mondrian and developments in modern architecture.

Architecture was perhaps the art form most closely connected in the public mind with the regime. The imposing neoclassical, colonnaded public buildings of Marcello Piacentini, the architect favored by the regime who had been associated with the influential *Novecento* movement, epitomized fascism in the public mind. The Fascists paid little attention to the human scale in their major architectural and urban renewal projects, such as the reworking of the area around the Colosseum and the Fori Imperiali in Rome, where the medieval quarter was sacrificed, families displaced, and numerous archeological treasures lost to highlight a few ruins and to build an avenue suitable only for the regime's grotesque public displays. Similar errors were committed in the reconstruction of the area around the Tomb of Augustus and with the Via della Conciliazione leading to the Vatican and in the urban renewal projects which reshaped Piazza San Babila or the Duomo piazza in Milan. The sole benefits of all this were reaped by the old urban propertied elites and Fascist newcomers who built their fortunes in land speculation. (Significantly, every governor of Rome during the Fascist era, except for Bottai, came from the aristocracy.)

But just as in the case of painting, the Fascists never completely opted for a single style. International styles, formulated by the Bauhaus and Le Corbusier, influenced the Italians. Beginning in the late 1920s rationalist architects (Adalberto Libera, Giuseppe Terragni, Luigi Figini, Carlo Enrico Rava, and Giuseppe Pagano) began to make their name by challenging the neoclassical style. In 1931 at the second exposition of the Italian Movement for Rationalist Architecture, the modernists even put together a photo exhibit which attacked the work of officially favored architects. Then, instead of a condemnation, they were invited to play a major role in the tremendously successful 1932 Mostra della Rivoluzione Fascista (Exhibition of the Fascist Revolution). This event, seen by well over three million visitors, retold the history of Italy from World War I to the seizure of power and the triumph of the Duce. It brought together artists and architects representing a variety of modern styles from the Bauhaus to Russian constructivism for the task of designing the various rooms; the Rationalist architect Giuseppe Terragni was put in charge of the all-important room for 1922.

What took place after 1932 was a fusion of styles. Major figures like Piacentini accepted aspects of the modern movement, and during the 1930s rationalist architecture dominated the construction of much private housing and of local party headquarters, notably Terragni's Casa del Fascio of Como. The new cities of Italy and its colonies, such as Sabaudia and Aprilia which were established for internal colonization projects, reflected this fusion of styles, as did the satellite city that Mussolini envisaged for the ill-fated Esposizione Universale di Roma (EUR), which stands today as a monument to the best and worst of Fascist architecture.

A second group which would have resisted direct control was the cultural apparatus created by the Catholic Church. Throughout the 1930s the failure of the regime to provide a set of compelling ideals left an opening for a religious revival. Catholic culture did not so much challenge the regime as define fascism in a way that was compatible with religious faith. Rarely, except during the conflict over Catholic youth organizations in 1931, did disputes become open, but the Church gave little ground in the cultural war. In 1934 Gentile's works were placed on the Index of Forbidden Books. The Catholics ensured that they would have a voice in the new *Italian Encyclopedia* in all areas touching on religion. Profascist Catholics, who published in journals like the Florentine *Frontespizio*, denied an independent moral basis for fascism and rejected the notion that the state was the source of all values, even while they operated within the framework of the regime.

Catholic passive resistance stiffened a bit during the racial campaign of 1938. Even more important were Catholic suspicions about the appropriation of religious symbols and rituals by totalitarian and neopagan currents within fascism which gained ground as a result of the alliance with Nazi Germany during the late 1930s. In reaction, Catholics tended to stress ever more forcefully the autonomous activities of Catholic Action and the Catholic university and diocesan organizations.

A final source of potential resistance to cultural dictation was the generation of intellectuals who matured artistically within the regime. For those in or just leaving the universities during the 1930s, the cultural heroes of the first decades of the century were mere names. D'Annunzio was no longer a source of inspiration, and Gentile was under assault from both Catholics and Fascist radicals. The paucity of content that was transmitted by official organs after 1935 emphasized the void left by the passing of the pre-1914 generation. Benedetto Croce's prestige was untouched, but he seemed a distant figure to a generation that had been educated to believe that the liberal tradition was dead. The opponents of fascism in exile often lost touch with the country; censorship kept their views and activities from reaching the majority of Italians. That extraordinary generation of young writers—Vasco Pratolini, Romano Bilenchi, Cesare Pavese, Vitaliano Brancati, and Elio Vittorini—looked to modern American and European literature and film for inspiration. In politics they sought a social and political philosophy which would live up to the expectations that they had earlier placed in corporativism.

Even among those young Fascists—Berto Ricci, Edgardo Sulis, and the *L'Universale* group or Niccolo Giani of the Scuola di Mistica Fascista—who sincerely believed in the promises of the regime, there was no real respect for the system as it actually existed during the late 1930s. They dreamed of a new and uncorrupted fascism to be realized on a European-wide scale in alliance (and also in competition) with Nazi Germany.

In the face of obvious youth disillusionment, Bottai's cultural alternative attempted to offer something to the apolitical artists and writers, Catholics, and the modernist or youth culture. In 1940 he instituted the Bergamo Prize as a pluralistic counterweight to Farinacci's Cremona award. The Ministry of National Education expanded the competence of the Superintendency of Fine Arts to include the entire architectural and artistic patrimony from the Roman to the contemporary era. (Unfortunately, Bottai, as governor of Rome, was himself responsible for some of the attacks on the architectural patrimony of that city.) But the most far-reaching effort to win over higher culture by a carrot rather than a stick came with *Primato*, an elegantly produced political-literary review, begun by Bottai in 1940. Young intellectuals like Carlo Emilio

Gadda, Vitaliano Brancati, Cesare Pavese, Mario Alicata, and
Giaime Pintor, who were making the transition from Fascist dis-
sidence to overt antifascism, wrote for *Primato* alongside stalwarts
of the regime. It was, however, too late to rally intellectuals to the
"national" rather than the "fascist" war. Unlike 1914 and 1915,
when the universities were swept by patriotic fervor, most intellectuals in 1940 simply could not be convinced that, in its hour of
need, the regime had any legitimacy.

Fascist cultural policy was the inevitable result of the method
of rule which Mussolini applied to politics and economics. The
regime would allow no single ideological or cultural perspective
to emerge. Instead of a monolithic system, various fiefdoms were
created, Gentile shaped the *Italian Encyclopedia* and the fascist Institutes of Culture and influenced the Sansoni, LeMonnier, and
La Nuova Italia publishing houses, as well as numerous journals
and philosophical associations. The Catholics had their university in Milan, the Federation of Catholic University Students, and
a network of papers and cultural reviews like the Florentine
Frontespizio. Fascist cultural militants controlled Berto Ricci's
L'Universale and Alessandro Pavolini's *Il Bargello*, as well as many
of the reviews of the Fascist University Groups. The tolerated opposition contributed to Croce's *La Critica* and to Luigi Einaudi's
Rivista di Storia Economica or published with the Einaudi or Laterza
presses. Young critics of the regime had small reviews like the
Milanese *Corrente di Vita Giovanile* in which they tried to define a
modernist and European cultural alternative. The pro-Nazis and
anti-Semites expressed themselves through papers like Telesio
Interlandi's *Il Tevere* and *Difesa della Razza* and the review
Quadrivio. The universities and academies provided a refuge for
the apolitical intellectuals who accepted the regime and hoped
that it would not make too many impositions on them. Different
prizes and expositions existed for various schools of art, just as
projects were divided between rationalist architects and their opponents.

An unintended side benefit of this confusion was that the Fascist regime did not disrupt the continuity of Italian culture, even
during the racial campaign, to the same extent that the Nazis did

in Germany. Most Italian intellectuals applied a high degree of self-censorship (bad in itself) but nothing more. By allowing autonomy for avant-garde, traditional and Catholic culture, the regime tolerated competing models. When the time came, these cultural fiefdoms were able to retreat to their basic loyalties and beliefs in order to survive the collapse of the regime. An even greater flaw from any Fascist totalitarian perspective was the failure to offer a set of valid political or social ideals to the young. Here again, the way was left open for competing models—American, communist, Catholic—which were independent of the regime. By 1940 fascism was associated with an aging, cynical, weary group of politicians. It sought rejuvenation in a war whose terms were set by Nazi Germany and whose outcome, either victory or defeat, meant the end of the system of rule that had been established by Mussolini from 1922 to 1940.

Chapter Eleven
Conclusion

Fascism developed out of a general crisis of the political and social system connected with the rise of the mass participation state
during and just after World War I. This mass participation state as
it emerged in the early decades of the twentieth century was
marked by four features: universal suffrage or, at least, universal
male suffrage; a high degree of mass mobilization, initially by
left-wing organizations; new social and economic demands put
forward by democratic and revolutionary mass organizations; and,
finally, a nineteenth-century legacy of poorly fragmented middle-
class political organizations that strained to compete against socialist or communist movements. Traditional liberal individualism and faith in the free market appeared pallid alternatives in
the rush to organize the newly politicized and enfranchised
masses, especially in contrast to potent revolutionary myths of
working class solidarity and liberation. Fascism exploded on the
scene as an alternative to liberalism and socialism—a mass movement of the middle class and a party through which important
economic and political interest groups sought to preserve the economic and social status quo in difficult times. The original nucleus
of 1919, composed of former socialists and syndicalists, contributed a passion for violent revolutionary change and an understanding of mass organizations. They were joined between 1919
and 1921 by provincial middle-class veterans, students, and young
professionals, who saw the movement as a vehicle to acquire
higher social and political status. Eventually, they would find in

the single party and the Fascist corporative and social welfare system both an outlet for their ambitions and a means to attempt controlled modernization without social upheaval. These various components united in their desire to break the hold of the Socialist party and unions over a substantial sector of the working class and to substitute the Fascist party as the link between the political class and the mass base.

To achieve these ambitions, fascism, as a broad, middle-class movement, had to come to terms with the dominant social and economic interest groups of Italy: industry, large-scale agriculture, the monarchy, the Catholic Church, and the military. Beginning with the landowners, important segments of the established order entered the Fascist movement and created their own version of fascism. By the time that the movement transformed itself into a political party in 1921, it was already a heterogeneous coalition and would become increasingly so after the March on Rome, when large numbers of conservatives flocked to the winning side. Thus, any effort to seek in the radical Fascist program of 1919 the true essence of the movement runs up against the reality that Mussolini's first leftist and nationalist fascism was a total failure. Once transformed into a mass party of the middle class, the Fascist movement found it impossible to return to the supposed purity of its radical origins.

Fascism *as regime* opted for an essentially conservative solution to the complicated problem of distributing power, especially after Mussolini was forced to concede ground to the conservatives during the Matteotti crisis of 1924. The ability of the conservative allies of fascism to entrench themselves stands in marked contrast to Hitler's ability to purge his conservative allies within months of assuming power. In 1925 and 1926 Mussolini rejected the primacy of the Fascist party, as demanded by the provincial extremists. Instead, the party was subjugated to the state bureaucracy and to the necessities of compromise with conservative power centers and forced into a long-term strategy of slow infiltration of Fascist militants into the traditional civil service. Mussolini gave *de facto* recognition to "hyphenated fascism" by setting up a series of fiefdoms in economics, politics, and culture.

The Duce moved by no preconceived plan. He responded to events and, with great tactical skill and some luck, turned them to his advantage. The regime proceeded on this course by trial and error, although its solutions were inevitably statist, authoritarian, and nationalist.

The history of the Fascist regime can be seen as a period of consolidation from 1922 to 1935 and as a period of disintegration from 1936 to 1943. Consolidation of power was a long and uneven process, and the disintegration of the regime was imperceptible at first and never inevitable until Mussolini opted for war in June 1940. During the 1920s the Fascist regime quite willingly compromised with the economic and social structures of the prefascist era. The government limited its role to the reorganization of the political class, the elimination of opposition alternatives, and the creation of new links between the state and the masses by means of the Fascist party's monopoly over political life.

Two options presented themselves to the Fascist regime with the onset of the depression in 1929. The "corporative" alternative demanded that the regime challenge the agreements made earlier and force the banking and industrial bailout to take place within the newly created structures of the corporative state. Many young, technocratic-minded Fascists wanted a system of comprehensive state planning in which the corporative bureaucracy would hold the balance between labor and management, but any such course meant a challenge to the established economic order.

Instead, Mussolini chose the "conservative" option, which established parallel economic structures; the corporative institutions busily spun their wheels and went nowhere, while real economic choices were made either through new noncorporative institutions or by direct negotiations between government and industry. In 1933 the state took over a large part of the banking system, as well as important sectors of heavy industry. Whole branches of the productive system were reorganized between 1933 and 1939 under the Istituto per la Ricostruzione Industriale Industriale (IRI) and state-sponsored cartels. In this vast undertaking Mussolini ignored the corporative "third way" between capitalism and socialism in favor of a continuation of the basic alliances established during the 1920s. The result was an intensification of the military-industrial complex with some loss of autonomy by the economic fiefdoms in favor of the state. Though not always to the same extent, similar developments took place throughout Europe and America during the depression years. Thus, fascism did not create its own unique economic system but rather grafted further statist and bureaucratic tissue on the existing body of Italian capitalism.

The rise of Adolf Hitler had a double influence on Italian fascism. Until 1933 Italy had served as the sole model for authoritarian movements. The assumption of power by the Nazis in January of that year challenged this monopoly by providing direct competition for leadership of the growing antidemocratic movement in Europe. Just as the regime drained all real content from its own ideology, the Fascists began to propose fascism as a universal solution to the problems facing a depression-ridden continent. But the totalitarian dynamism of the Nazi regime also exposed to many Fascists the relative backwardness of their own system. The Italian stress on propaganda, mass mobilization, and racial policy during the thirties must be seen both as a response to this growing Nazi challenge and as a need to mobilize the country for greater challenges in foreign policy. However, when Mussolini was forced to act in this new competitive climate, he found that the Fascist system simply could not respond as he wished. Economic backwardness, bureaucratic rigidities, and the restrictions imposed by earlier compromises with established interests hobbled Italy in its alliance with Nazi Germany. The result was a deepening conflict between the totalitarian, antibourgeois, and pseudorevolutionary rhetoric of the regime and the realities of Italy during the late 1930s.

It was mainly in the area of foreign policy that Hitler created conditions which destabilized the conservative orientation of the Fascist regime. As the European diplomatic order began to crumble, Mussolini found himself freer from the constraints of the balance of power and of the cautious policy of the Foreign Ministry. International crisis and war, in turn, provided an opportunity to subordinate domestic policy, where the Duce had less freedom to maneuver, to foreign policy, and to a personal drive for prestige and power. His long-term goal was to undo the compromises worked out earlier with the conservative fiefdoms and to create a new Fascist generation by remaking Italians. Everything depended on success in foreign and military policy. Here again, however, the results were less than satisfactory. By 1936 Italy had lost the leadership of the bloc of revisionist states in the Danubian basin to Germany. The Duce's efforts to shift the center of foreign policy to the Mediterranean led him into risky ventures in Ethiopia and Spain, toward war with England and France, and into increasing dependence on his German ally. Fascist illusions of an independent "parallel war" to that waged by Nazi Germany collapsed in Greece and North Africa in late 1940 and early 1941.

During the 1930s the Fascist regime became more dependent on the myth of Mussolini. The Duce was a highly intelligent and resourceful politician, but he too became enmeshed in his own image. Mussolini had always been mistrustful and cynical in dealing with subordinates. The death of his brother, Arnaldo, and his growing isolation from old political associates reinforced some of the Duce's negative character traits. Mussolini's own reading of Oswald Spengler, Richard Korherr, and other deeply pessimistic writers of the 1920s convinced him of the coming crisis of civilization and of the dangers of demographic stagnation and inevitable economic and military decline. In the twilight of civilization a few heroic figures might stand against the tide. This sense of destiny began to cloud his judgment. He had, after all, been correct in predicting that Italy could defy Europe in its seizure of Ethiopia. He then reacted scornfully to military and economic advisers who told him that the country did not have the means to fight a major war in 1940. Even when Mussolini could not completely ignore reality, the failures of the present drove him to try to stake the destiny of the regime on the creation of that elusive, truly Fascist future generation. Mussolini, like the pilot of a crashing airplane, reached for controls that no longer responded to his touch.

Discontent grew slowly after 1938 among Catholics, young intellectuals, some industrialists, and politicians, but, despite complaints, the Fascist system remained a satisfactory arrangement for the distribution of power, until defeat in war forced each part of the Fascist coalition to retreat within its own base. The coup which toppled Mussolini was largely a conservative effort to maintain the essentials of the system but without the erratic leadership of the Duce by coming to terms with the Allies. The later Italian Social Republic represented a counterattack by those Fascist extremists and proto-Nazis who were excluded from the benefits of the July 1943 coup against Mussolini. A much reduced group of Fascist fanatics, racists, and syndicalists tried to re-create the regime without the participation of the conservative institutional forces—church, monarchy, industry, and army—which now counted on the British and Americans to save them.

With these considerations in mind, the question of the relevance of Fascist ideology must be approached with caution. While the 1919 Fascist *movement* was led by many who began their careers in socialist and syndicalist politics and adopted collectivist social and economic programs, mass organizations, and populist rhetoric associated with the left, the *regime* moved in a conservative direction by using these innovative techniques of mass rule in order to save the social and economic status quo. Despite its rhetoric, the Fascist regime never disturbed social hierarchies and only tampered with private property under the impact of the depression; even then, nationalization of banking and heavy industry developed out of the logic of earlier policies and was carried out by the IRI without conflicting with private interests. Therefore, fascism was a rightist solution to the problem of organizing a mass participation state and of achieving controlled development. The aspirations of fascism's middle-class constituencies were realized within the established order, not against it.

The Fascist glorification of the state was totalitarian in the sense that the nation-state was the framework for all public initiatives and each individual was subordinate to it. Many of the measures taken by the Fascist regime to regulate private conduct, not only the vile racial legislation but also silly things like the abolition of *lei* and the imposition of the Fascist salute, were designed to break down the barrier between the public and private spheres. However, the inability of the Fascist state to penetrate the sphere of private life thwarted the attainment of the totalitarian state. The impact on the average Italian of the mass rallies and the efforts to create a secular religion around the state simply cannot be measured accurately in an authoritarian society. Fascism's rapid collapse and the remarkable strength of prefascist loyalties indicate that the regime had limited success in its totalitarian aspirations. Thus, interpretations that highlight fascism's socialist and syndicalist origins in order to develop a theory of left-wing fascism or those that stress fascism's efforts to create a new type of Italian by means of mass mobilization and the sacralization of politics should not necessarily be dismissed but need to be treated cautiously and measured against economic, social, and political realities. By the late 1930s the compromises that had stabilized fascism and had built a passive consensus were put under great stress. The logic of the Nazi alliance, the determination of the Fascist intransigents to move the regime in a totalitarian direction, and the growing impatience of the Duce made a crisis of the regime inevitable. The antibourgeois, collectivist, and totalitarian rhetoric during the 1930s indicated that Mussolini wanted to steer the regime in a new direction. War offered a chance to do this. But the very means to the end—the alliance with Nazi Germany and entry into World War II—proved fatal. There was no room for an autonomous Fascist Italy in a Nazi-dominated Europe.

Bibliographical Essay

This bibliography of Italian fascism is designed primarily to indicate the sources which proved valuable in the preparation of the several editions of this book. While it cannot in any way claim to be complete, it is a starting point for those who wish to do further work on particular aspects of Italian fascism. Emphasis has been placed on new material, even at the cost of omitting some older classics which figure in most bibliographies.

The best and most comprehensive introduction to the general subject of fascism is Stanley Payne's *A History of Fascism 1914–1945* (Madison: University of Wisconsin Press, 1995). Also useful is Roger Griffin's *The Nature of Fascism* (London: Routledge, 1994), which argues that fascism is a myth of national or racial rebirth. Griffin has also compiled a sourcebook: *Fascism* (Oxford: Oxford University Press, 1995). Alan Cassels's older *Fascism* (New York: Crowell, 1975) divides the subject into a fascism of controlled development, such as existed in Italy, and a more backward-looking model, of which Nazi Germany is a prime example. Close in outlook to the views expressed in my interpretation is John Weiss's *The Fascist Tradition* (New York: Harper and Row, 1967). In organizing my material, I was influenced by the writings of three early Marxists: Guido Aquila (Djula Saš), *Der Faschismus in Italien* (1923); Palmiro Togliatti, "A proposito del fascismo," (August 1928); and Richard Lowenthal, "Der Fascismus," (September–October 1935). Each appears in the excellent anthology compiled by Renzo De Felice, *Il fascismo: Le interpretazioni dei contemporanei e degli storici*

(Bari: Laterza, 1970). For a lively survey of recent scholarship and historical controversies, see Richard J. B. Bosworth, *The Italian Dictatorship: Problems and Perspectives in the Interpretation of Mussolini and Fascism* (London: Arnold, 1998). Guido Dorso's *Dittatura, classe politica e classe dirigente* (Turin: Einaudi, 1949), and Antonio Gramsci's *Note sul Machiavelli* (Rome: Riuniti, 1971) and *Gli intellettuali e l'organizzazione della cultura* (Turin: Einaudi, 1966) shaped my views on the political class and intermediate elites. Philip Morgan's recent *Italian Fascism 1919–1945* (New York: St. Martin's, 1995) is a concise survey of the history of the regime. A new collaborative effort to restate and update classical antifascist historiography in contrast to De Felicean revisionism is seen in Angelo Del Boca, Massimo Legnani, and Mario G. Rossi's *Il regime fascista* (Bari: Laterza, 1995). Angelo Tasca's *The Rise of Italian Fascism* (New York: Fertig, 1966), written in the 1930s, remains today the fundamental work on the rise of Italian fascism between 1919 and 1922. Pier Giorgio Zunino's *L'ideologia del fascismo: Miti, credenze e valori nella stabilizzazione del regime* (Bologna: Mulino, 1985) combines an acute explanation of the ideas behind fascism with an understanding of how these ideas penetrated the Italian consciousness. The *Historical Dictionary of Fascist Italy* (Westport, Conn.: Greenwood, 1982), edited by Philip Cannistraro, is a standard reference work for those interested in Fascist Italy.

Liberal Italy and the Rise of Fascism

The best general survey of liberal Italy is Christopher Seton Watson's *Italy from Liberalism to Fascism* (London: Meuthen, 1967). Recent treatments of Italian economic developments are by the Marxist historian Valerio Castronovo, "La storia economica," in *Storia d'Italia*, vol. 4, *Dall'unità a oggi* (Turin: Einaudi, 1975); by the late Rosario Romeo, who wrote from a liberal perspective, in *Breve storia della grande industria in Italia* (Bologna: Cappelli, 1961); by Vera Zamagni, *The Economic History of Italy, 1860–1990* (Oxford: Oxford University Press, 1993); and Gianni Toniolo, *Storia economica della Italia liberale 1850–1918* (Bologna: Il Mulino 1988).

On the interaction between politics and economics, see Giorgio Candeloro, *Storia dell'Italia moderna*, vol. 7, *La crisi del fine secolo e l'età giolittiana* (Milan: Feltrinelli, 1974); Frank J. Coppa, *Planning, Protectionism and Politics in Liberal Italy* (Washington, D.C.: Catholic University Press, 1971); and Douglas Forsyth, *The Crisis of Liberal Italy: Monetary and Financial Policy, 1914–1922* (Cambridge: Cambridge University Press, 1993), who offers an interesting analysis of the competing economic, social, and political interests faced by liberal governments.

On Mussolini's early life, the fundamental study remains Renzo De Felice's *Mussolini il rivoluzionario* (Turin: Einaudi, 1966). A. James Gregor's *Young Mussolini and the Intellectual Origins of Fascism* (Berkeley: University of California Press, 1979) takes Mussolini's socialism quite seriously, but the standard in English is still Gaudens Megaro, *Mussolini in the Making* (Boston: Houghton Mifflin, 1938). The best biography of Mussolini in English is by Denis Mack Smith, *Mussolini* (New York: Knopf, 1982).

On the various traditions which went into fascism, see Walter Adamson's *Avant-garde Florence: From Modernism to Fascism* (Cambridge: Harvard University Press, 1993) on the contribution of Florentine intellectuals around the review *La voce*; for syndicalism, David Roberts, *The Syndicalist Tradition and Italian Fascism* (Chapel Hill: University of North Carolina Press, 1979); for nationalism, Franco Gaeta, *Il nazionalismo italiano* (Naples: Edizioni Scientifiche Italiane, 1965), and A. J. De Grand, *The Italian Nationalist Association and the Rise of Fascism in Italy* (Lincoln: University of Nebraska Press, 1978); an overall picture of the ideological origins is given in Emilio Gentile, *Le origini dell'ideologia fascista* (Bari: Laterza, 1975).

The war and the immediate postwar crisis are covered by Piero Melograni, *Storia politica della Grande guerra* (Bari: Laterza, 1966) and Roberto Vivarelli, *Il dopoguerra in Italia: Dalla fine della guerra all'impresa di Fiume* (Naples: Ricciardi, 1967) and his recent second volume *Storia delle origini del fascismo: L'Italia dalla grande guerra alla marcia su Roma* (Bologna: Il Mulino, 1991), which covers events from late 1919 to the end of 1920.

Much research has been done on the social problems that pro-

duced fascism. Notable are the pioneering study by Marzio
Barbagli, *Educating for Unemployment: Politics, Labor Markets, and
the School System-Italy, 1859–1973* (New York: Columbia University Press, 1982), which traces the impact of unemployment among
professionals, and Paolo Sylos Labini, *Saggio sulle classi sociali* (Bari:
Laterza, 1975). On the veterans, see Giovanni Sabbatucci, *I
combattenti nel primo dopoguerra* (Bari: Laterza, 1974). The early
Fascist electorate and political personnel is Jens Petersen's subject in "Elettorato e base sociale del fascismo italiano negli anni
venti," *Studi storici* 16 (1975): 627–69; Paolo Farnetti, "La crisi della
democrazia italiana e l'avvento del fascismo, 1919–1922," *Rivista
italiana di Scienza Politica* 5 (1975): 45–82; Marco Revelli, "Italy," in
The Social Base of European Fascist Movements, ed. Detlef Mühlberger
(London: Croon Helm, 1987); and in a comparative context, Juan
Linz, "Some Notes toward a Comparative Study of Fascism in a
Sociological Historical Perspective," *Fascism: A Reader's Guide*, ed.
Walter Lacqueur (Berkeley: University of California Press, 1976).

Several studies in English of the rise of fascism in various provinces have appeared. Each reveals the particular balance between
rural elites and the lower middle class which provided the base
for the Fascist movement. Paul Corner's *Fascism in Ferrara* (Oxford: Oxford University Press, 1974) and Anthony Cardoza's
*Agrarian Elites and Italian Fascism: The Province of Bologna, 1901–
1926* (Princeton: Princeton University Press, 1982) study two key
provinces which led the way in the rural reaction against socialism. Alice Kelikian's *Town and Country under Fascism: The Transformation of Brescia, 1915–1926* (Oxford: Oxford University Press,
1986) looks at the balanced agricultural-industrial zone which was
the home province of future party secretary Augusto Turati. Frank
Snowden's *Fascism and the Great Estates in the South of Italy: Apulia,
1902–1922* (Cambridge: Cambridge University Press, 1986) deals
with the naked agrarian reaction in one of the most evolved provinces of the South. Other major studies on particular provinces
are: Elio Apih, *Italia, fascismo e antifascismo in Venezia Giulia* (Bari:
Laterza, 1966); Rolando Cavandoli, *Le origini del fascismo a Reggio
Emilia* (Rome: Riuniti, 1972); Andrea Binazzi and Ivo Guasti, eds.,
La Toscana nel regime fascista (Florence: Olschki, 1971); Simona

Colarizzi, *Dopoguerra e fascismo in Puglia* (Bari: Laterza, 1971); and Raffaele Colapietra, *Napoli tra dopoguerra e fascismo* (Milan: Feltrinelli, 1962).

The only complete study of the PNF is the older one by Dante Germino, *The Italian Fascist Party in Power* (Minneapolis: University of Minnesota Press, 1959), but Emilio Gentile has published the first volume of his comprehensive study of the party, *Storia del Partito fascista, 1919–1922* (Bari: Laterza, 1989); also by the same author is *La via italiana al totalitarismo: Il partito e lo Stato nel regime fascista* (Rome: La Nuova Italia Scientifica, 1995). The best complete study of the March on Rome is Antonino Repaci's *La Marcia su Roma: Mito e realtà* (Milan: Rizzoli, 1972).

The Fascist Regime

Any serious reader must consult the following volumes by Renzo De Felice: *Mussolini il fascista*, vol. 2, *L'organizzazione dello stato fascista* (Turin: Einaudi, 1968); *Mussolini il Duce: Gli anni del consenso, 1929–1935* (Turin: Einaudi, 1974); *Mussolini il Duce: Lo stato totalitario, 1936–1940* (Turin: Einaudi, 1981); and *Mussolini l'alleato*, 2 vols. (Turin: Einaudi, 1990), which carries the biography of Mussolini to 1943. The final volume on the Italian Social Republic was not completed before Professor De Felice's death. The late Alberto Aquarone's *L'organizzazione dello stato totalitario* (Turin: Einaudi, 1965) is the most complete guide to the institutional arrangements of fascism to 1939; Claudio Schwarzemberg, *Diritto e giustizia nell'Italia fascista* (Milan: Mursia, 1977) covers the legal framework. Mariuccia Salvati has studied the impact of fascism on middle-class state employees in *Il regime e gli impiegati: La nazionalizzazione piccolo-borghese nel ventennio fascista* (Bari: Laterza, 1992). Guido Melis has contrasted the bureaucratic systems in liberal and fascist Italy in *Due modelli di amministrazione tra liberalismo e fascismo* (Rome: Ministero per i Bene Culturali, 1988). Edward Tannenbaum's *The Fascist Experience: Society and Culture, 1922–1945* (New York: Basic Books, 1972) attempts to bring together all aspects of the regime in a single volume. Adrian

Lyttelton's *Seizure of Power* (Princeton: Princeton University Press, 1987) is the best work on fascism from 1922 to 1929 in any language.

Several studies have appeared recently which deal with fascism's efforts at totalitarian mobilization. The most important is Emilio Gentile, *The Sacralization of Politics* (Cambridge: Harvard University Press, 1996). Other interesting studies along the same lines are Mabel Berezin, *Making the Fascist Self: The Political Culture of Interwar Italy* (Ithaca: Cornell University Press, 1997), and Simonetta Falasca Zamponi, *Fascist Spectacle: The Aesthetics of Power in Mussolini's Italy* (Berkeley: University of California Press, 1997). Two recent attempts to draw parallels between Fascist and Nazi experience are Richard Bissel, ed., *Fascist Italy and Nazi Germany: Comparisons and Contrasts* (Cambridge: Cambridge University Press, 1996), and A. J. De Grand, *Fascist Italy and Nazi Germany: The Fascist Style of Rule* (London: Routledge, 1995).

By now, all the special interests which formed the Fascist regime have received study. For the Catholic Church, see Richard Webster, *The Cross and the Fasces* (Stanford: Stanford University Press, 1960); Peter Kent, *The Pope and the Duce: The International Impact of the Lateran Agreements* (London: Macmillan, 1981); J. F. Pollard, *The Vatican and Italian Fascism, 1929–1932* (Cambridge: Cambridge University Press, 1985); Francesco Margiotta Broglio, *Italia e Santa Sede dalla Grande Guerra alla Conciliazione* (Bari: Laterza, 1967); and Jone Gaillard, "The Attraction of Fascism for the Church of Rome," in John Milfull, *The Attraction of Fascism: Social Psychology and the Aesthetic of the Triumph of the Right* (New York: Berg, 1990). John Whittam, *The Politics of the Italian Army* (Hamden, Conn.: Archon Books, 1971), Giorgio Rochat's *L'esercito italiano da Vittorio Veneto a Mussolini* (Bari: Laterza, 1967) and "L'esercito e fascismo," in *Fascismo e società*, ed. Guido Quazza, (Turin: Einaudi, 1975) cover civil-military relations.

On industry and economic policy, see Piero Melograni, *Gli industriali e Mussolini* (Milan: Longanesi, 1972); Roland Sarti, *Fascism and the Industrial Leadership in Italy* (Berkeley: University of California Press, 1971); Mario Abbrate, *La lotta sindacale nella industrializzazione dell'Italia, 1906–1926* (Turin: L'Impresa, 1966);

Franklin H. Adler, *Italian Industrialists from Liberalism to Fascism* (Cambridge: Cambridge University Press, 1995); Salvatore Della Francesca, *La politica economica del fascismo* (Bari: Laterza, 1978); G. M. Rey, "Una sintesi dell'economia italiana durante il fascismo," in *L'economia italiana, 1860–1940*, ed. G. Toniolo (Bari: Laterza, 1978); and Ester Fano Damascelli, "La restaurazione antifascista liberista: Ristagno e sviluppo economico durante il fascismo," in *Movimento di liberazione in Italia* 23 (1971): 47–99. The special issue of the journal *Quarderni storici* 10 (May–December 1975) contains two important articles on industrial development: Pierluigi Ciocca, "L'Italia nell'economia mondiale, 1922–1940," pp. 324–76, and G. Tattara and Gianni Toniolo, "Lo sviluppo industriale italiano tra le due guerre," pp. 377–437. On the tension between the warlike policies of the regime and the interests of investors and small savers, see Giuseppe Maione, *L'imperialismo straccione: Classi sociali e finanza di guerra dall'impresa etiopica al conflitto mondiale* (Bologna: Il Mulino, 1979). Finally, there is the excellent treatment of the Italian economy, written around 1940 by Pietro Griffone, an official of the Confindustria and clandestine member of the Italian Communist Party: *Il capitale finanziario in Italia.* 2d ed. (Turin: Einaudi, 1971).

On more specialized subjects, see Jon S. Cohen, "La rivalutazione della lira del 1927," in Toniolo, ed., *L'economia italiana* (cited above); Roland Sarti, "Mussolini and the Industrial Leadership in the Battle of the Lira," *Past and Present* (May 1970): 97–112; Paul Corner, "Italy," in *The Working Class and Politics in Europe and America, 1929–1945*, eds. Stephen Salter and John Stevenson (London: Longmans, 1990), for the impact of fascist policies on the working class; and the biography by Sergio Romano, *Giuseppe Volpi: Industria e finanza tra Giolitti e Mussolini* (Milan: Bompiani, 1979). The former minister of foreign exchange and trade, Felice Guarneri, wrote two volumes of memoirs, *Battaglie economiche tra le due grandi guerre*, 2 vols. (Milan: Garzanti, 1953), and Alberto Pirelli's notebooks have been published: *Taccuini, 1922–1943*, ed. Donato Barbone (Bologna: Il Mulino, 1984). For an overview of Italian agriculture, see Domenico Preti, "La politica agraria del fascismo," *Studi storici* 14 (1973): 802–69; Ester Fano, "Problemi e vicende dell'agricoltura tra le due guerre," A. Cadeddu, S. Lepre, F. Socrete, "Ristagno e sviluppo nel settore agricolo italiano, 1918–1939," and Paul Corner, "Considerazoni sull'agricoltura capitalistica durante il fascismo," all in *Quaderni storici* 10 (May–December 1975): 468–96, 497–18, 519–29; Paul Corner, "Agricoltura e industria durante il fascismo," *Problemi del socialismo* 4 (1972): 721–45; Jon S. Cohen, "Fascism and Agriculture in Italy: Policies and Consequences," *Economic History Review* 32 (February 1979): 70–87.

Social Policies and Living Standards

Fascist social and labor policies are the subject of Ferdinando Cordova, *Le origini dei sindacati fascisti, 1918–1926* (Bari: Laterza, 1974); Bruno Uva, *La nascita dello stato corporativa e sindacale fascista* (Assisi: Carucci, n.d.); Claudio Schwarzemberg, *Il sindacalismo fascista* (Milan: Mursia, 1972); Roland Sarti, "I sindacati fascisti e la politica economica del regime," *Problemi del socialismo* 14 (September–December 1972): 746–65; Vera Zamagni, "La dinamica dei salari nel settore industriale, 1921–1931," *Quaderni storici* 10 (May–December 1975): 530–49; and Gian Carlo Jocteau, *La magistratura e i conflitti di lavoro durante il fascismo* (Milan: Feltrinelli, 1978). Social and labor studies are also featured in several important works by Victoria De Grazia: "La taylorizzazione del tempo libero nel regime fascista," *Studi storici* 19 (1978): 331–66; "Disciplina del lavoro e mediazione sociale sotto il regime fascista: Le funzione del Dopolavoro nell'organizzazione del lavoro," in Fondazione Giangiacomo Feltrinelli, *La classe operaia durante il fascismo. Annali della Fondazione Giangiacomo Feltrinelli 1979–80* (Milan: Feltrinelli, 1980); and *The Culture of Consent: Mass Organization of Leisure in Fascist Italy* (Cambridge: Cambridge University Press, 1981). A fine study that might easily be put under the section on women as well as on labor is Perry Willson, *The Clockwork Factory: Women and Work in Fascist Italy* (Oxford: Oxford University Press, 1993), which deals with the electrical firm Magnetti Marelli and its largely female labor force. Finally, the already mentioned volume of the *Annali Feltrinelli* for 1979–80 is entirely devoted to the standard of living and labor conditions under fascism. On the reception of fascism by workers in Turin, see Luisa Passerini, *Fascism in Popular Memory* (London: Cambridge University Press, 1987).

Women, Demography, and Race

Victoria De Grazia has published a fine, comprehensive study of Fascist policy toward women: *How Fascism Ruled Women* (Berkeley: University of California Press, 1992). Older studies are Franca Pieroni Bortolotti's *Femminismo e partiti politici in Italia, 1918–1926* (Rome: Riuniti, 1978); A. J. De Grand, "Women under Italian Fascism," *Historical Journal* 14 (December 1976): 947–68; Emiliana Noether, "Italian Women and Fascism: A Reevaluation," *Italian Quarterly* 23 (Fall 1982): 69–80; Lesley Caldwell, "Reproducers of the Nation: Women and the Family in Fascist Policy," in *Rethinking Italian Fascism*, ed. David Forgacs (London: Lawrence and Wishart, 1986).

Demographic policy has attracted much attention recently. Far and away the best book on the subject is Carl Ipsen's, *Dictating Demography: The Problem of Population in Fascist Italy* (Cambridge: Cambridge University Press, 1996). Other very useful works are Cecilia Dau Novelli, *Famiglia e modernizzazione in Italia tra le due guerre* (Rome: Edizioni Studium, 1994); David Horn, *Social Bodies: Science, Reproduction and Italian Modernity* (Princeton: Princeton University Press, 1994); Maria S. Quine, *Population Politics in Twentieth-Century Europe* (London: Routledge, 1996); and two studies by Denise Detragiache, "Un aspect de la politique demographique de l'Italie fasciste: La répression de l'avortement," *Mélanges de l'Ecole Française de Rome* (1980): 690–732, and "Le fascisme féminin de S. Sepolcro a l'affaire Matteotti," *Revue d'Histoire Moderne et Contemporaine* (July–September 1983), also in *Storia contemporanea* 13 (1983): 211–51.

Fascist racial policies have received ample coverage in Renzo De Felice, *Storia degli ebrei sotto il fascismo* (Turin: Einaudi, 1961); Meir Michaelis, *Mussolini and the Jews: German Italian Relations and the Jewish Question in Italy* (Oxford: Oxford University Press, 1978); Dan Vittorio Segre, *Memoirs of a Fortunate Jew: An Italian Story* (New York: Adler and Adler, 1987); Susan Zuccotti, *The Italians and the Holocaust: Persecution, Rescue and Survival* (New York: Basic Books, 1987); Michele Sarfatti, *Mussolini contro gli ebrei: Cronaca dell'elaborazione delle leggi del 1938* (Turin: Silivo Zamorani, Editore, 1994).

Foreign Policy

H. James Burgwyn has written a comprehensive study of Italian foreign policy from 1918 to 1940: *Italian Foreign Policy in the Interwar Period, 1918–1940* (Westport, Conn.: Greenwood Press, 1997). A number of books cover narrower topics: Giorgio Rumi, *Alle origini della politica estera fascista* (Bari: Laterza, 1968); Alan Cassels, *Mussolini's Early Diplomacy* (Princeton: Princeton University Press, 1970); G. Carocci, *La politica estera dell'Italia fascista, 1925–1928* (Bari: Laterza, 1969); Fulvio D'Amoja, *Declino e prima crisi dell'Europa di Versailles* (Milan: Giuffrè, 1967); Paolo Nello's biography of Dino Grandi, *Dino Grandi: La formazione di un leader fascista* (Bologna: Il Mulino, 1987), and *Un fedele disubbidiente: Dino Grandi da Palazzo Chigi al 25 luglio* (Bologna: Il Mulino, 1993); Fulvio Suvich, *Memorie, 1932–1936* (Milan: Rizzoli, 1984); George Baer, *The Coming of the Italo-Ethiopian War* (Cambridge: Harvard University Press, 1967); John Coverdale, *Italian Intervention in the Spanish Civil War* (Princeton: Princeton University Press, 1975); Rosario Quartararo, *Roma tra Londra e Berlino* (Rome: Bulzoni, 1975); Alberto Aquarone, "Lo spirito pubblico in Italia alla vigilia della Seconda Guerra Mondiale," *Nord e Sud* 11 (January 1964): 111–23; two important contributions by Macgregor Knox, *Mussolini Unleashed 1939–1941: Politics and Strategy in Fascist Italy's Last War* (Cambridge: Cambridge University Press, 1982), and "Conquest, Foreign and Domestic in Fascist Italy and Nazi Germany," *Journal of Modern History* 56 (March 1984): 1–57; F. W. Deakin, *Brutal Friendship* (New York: Harper and Row, 1962), are also important for the history of the Italian Social Republic.

On the collapse of the regime and the RSI, see Dino Grandi, *25 luglio: Quarant'anni dopo* (Bologna: Il Mulino, 1983); Giorgio Bocca, *Storia d'Italia nella guerra fascista* (Bari: Laterza, 1969) and *La Repubblica di Mussolini* (Bari: Laterza 1977). Claudio Pavone's *Una guerra civile* (Milan: Bollati Boringhieri, 1992) is a brilliant and pathbreaking work on the Resistance as a civil, class, and liberation struggle. The all-pervasive nature of the German occupation is described in Enzo Collotti, *L'amministrazione tedesca dell'Italia occupata* (Milan: Lerici, 1963), and in Lutz Klinkhammer, *L'occupazione tedesca in Italia, 1943–1945* (Milan: Bollati Boringhieri, 1993).

Culture, Education, and Generational Conflict

On the mentality of the generation that had been educated by the regime, see Ruggero Zangrandi, *Il lungo viaggio attraverso il fascismo* (Milan: Feltrinelli, 1964); Ettore Alberoni, E. Antonini, R. Palmieri, *La generazione degli anni difficili* (Bari: Laterza, 1962); Marina Addis Saba, *Gioventù italiana del littorio: La stampa dei giovani nella guerra fascista* (Milan: Feltrinelli, 1973); Ugoberto Alfassio Grimaldi and Marina Addis Saba, *Cultura a passo romano: Storia e strategie dei Littoriali della Cultura e dell'Arte* (Milan: Feltrinelli, 1983); Mario Sechi, *Il mito della nuova cultura: Giovani, realismo, e politica negli anni trenta* (Manduria: Lacaita, 1984); Daniele Marchesini, *La scuola dei gerarchi* (Milan: Feltrinelli, 1976); Domenico Carella, *Fascismo prima, fascismo dopo* (Rome: Armando, 1973), a memoir by one of the editors of the collectivist and socially oriented reviews, *Il Saggiatore* and *Il Cantiere*; Michael Ledeen, *Universal Fascism: The Theory and Practice of the Fascist International* (New York: Fertig, 1972).

There are a number of exceptional works on Fascist culture. Philip Cannistraro has contributed two essential studies: *La fabbrica del consenso: Fascismo e mass media* (Bari: Laterza, 1975), which dealt with the propaganda machinery, and with Brian Sullivan, *Il Duce's Other Woman: The Untold Story of Margherita Sarfatti, Benito Mussolini's Jewish Mistress* (New York: Morrow, 1993), which traces Sarfatti's role in setting cultural policy. Luisa Mangoni's *Interventismo nella cultura: Intellettuali e riviste del fascismo* (Bari:

Laterza, 1974) is a wide-ranging presentation of the aspirations and gradual disillusionment of the generations which created and, finally, abandoned fascism. On the methods by which the regime mobilized consent, see Marla Susan Stone, *The Patron State: Culture and Politics in Fascist Italy* (Princeton: Princeton University Press, 1998), an excellent examination of the cultural bureaucracy established by fascism; Mario Isnenghi, *Intellettuali militanti e intellettuali funzionari: Appunti sulla cultura fascista* (Turin: Einaudi, 1979); Marinella Ferrarotto, *L'Accademia d'Italia: Intellettuali e potere durante il fascismo* (Naples: Liguori, 1977); Giorgio Luti, *Cronache letterarie tra le due guerre, 1920–1940* (Bari: Laterza, 1966); Ruth Ben-Ghiat, "The Politics of Realism: *Corrente di vita giovanile* and the Youth Culture of the 1930s," *Stanford Italian Review* 8 (1990): 139–64, and "Fascism, Writing and Memory: The Realist Aesthetic in Italy, 1930–1950," *Journal of Modern History* 67 (1995): 627–65; and, finally, the excellent anthology *Primato, 1940–1943*, Luisa Mangoni, ed. (Bari: De Donato, 1977).

On the revival of Catholic culture, see G. Rossini, ed., *Modernismo, fascismo, comunismo: Aspetti e figure della cultura e della politica dei cattolici del '900* (Bologna: Il Mulino, 1972); Paolo Rafagni, *I clerico-fascisti: Le riviste dell'Università Cattolica negli anni del regime* (Florence: Cooperativa Editrice Universitaria, 1975); Renato Moro, *La formazione della classe dirigente cattolica, 1929–1937* (Bologna: Il Mulino, 1979); Paolo Pombeni, *Gruppo dossettiano e la fondazione della democrazia italiana, 1938–1948* (Bologna: Il Mulino, 1979); and Richard J. Wolff, *Between Pope and Duce: Catholic Students in Fascist Italy* (New York: Peter Lang, 1990).

On the technocratic aspects of fascism, see Alberto Aquarone, "Le aspirazioni tecnocratiche del primo fascismo," *Nord e sud* 11 (April 1964): 109–28; Camillo Pellizzi, *Una rivoluzione mancata* (Milan: Longanesi, 1949); and the previously cited work by De Grand, *Bottai e la cultura fascista*.

Policies toward the media can be found in a number of works. Cannistraro's *Fabbrica del consenso*, already cited, is the basic study. For all aspects of Italian culture during the 1930s, see the catalogue of the exposition, *Annitrenta: Arte e cultura in Italia* (Milan: Mazzotta–Comune di Milano, 1982). On film, see Jean A. Gill,

L'Italie de Mussolini et son cinema (Paris: Editions Henri Veyrier, 1985); M. Landy, *Fascism in Film* (Princeton: Princeton University Press, 1986); James Hay, *Popular Film Culture in Fascist Italy* (Bloomington: Indiana University Press, 1987); Gian Piero Brunetta, *Cinema italiano tra le due guerre: Fascismo e politica cinematografica* (Milan: Mursia, 1975); and Luigi Freddi, *Il cinema* (Rome: l'Arnia, 1949). On radio, see Franco Monteleone, *La radio italiana nel periodo fascista: Studio e documenti, 1922–1945* (Venice: Marsilio, 1976) and Alberto Monticone, *Il fascismo al microfono: Radio e politica in Italia, 1924–1945* (Rome: Edizioni Studium, 1978). For art, see the already cited work by Stone, *The Patron State*; Emily Braun, *Mario Sironi, 1919–1945: Art and Politics in Fascist Italy* (Cambridge: Cambridge University Press, 1999); and U. Silva, *Ideologia e arte del fascismo* (Milan: Mazzotta, 1973). On theater, see Alberto Cesare Alberti, *Il teatro nel fascismo* (Rome: Bulzoni 1974); E. Scarpolini, *Organizzazione teatrale e politica del teatro nell'Italia fascista* (Florence, La Nuova Italia, 1989); and Jeffrey T. Schnapp, *Staging Fascism: 18 BL and the Theater of Masses for Masses* (Stanford: Stanford University Press, 1996). On music, see Harvey Sachs, *Music in Fascist Italy* (New York: Norton, 1987), and Fiamma Nicolodi, *Musica e musicisti nel ventennio fascista* (Fiesole: Discanto Edizioni, 1984).

Architecture has been well studied: Dennis Doordan, *Building Modern Italy* (New York: Princeton Architectural Press, 1988); Richard Etlin, *Modernism in Italian Architecture, 1890–1940* (Cambridge: MIT Press, 1991); Ellen Ruth Shapiro, "Building under Mussolini" (Ph.D. dissertation, Yale University, 1985) (Ann Arbor: University Microfilms, 1986); Diane Ghirardo, *Destiny on the Land: New Communities in Interwar Italy and America* (Princeton: Princeton University Press, 1989).

Fascist educational policy was surveyed in an old, but still quite good, work by L. Minio Paluello, *Education in Fascist Italy* (London: Oxford University Press, 1946); the present standard is Tracy Koon, *Believe, Obey, Fight: Political Socialization of Youth in Fascist Italy, 1922–1943* (Chapel Hill: University of North Carolina Press, 1985), and Michel Ostenc, *La scuola italiana durante il fascismo* (Bari: Laterza, 1981). On the organization of youth, see Carmen Betti,

L'Opera Nazionale Balilla e l'educazione fascista (Florence: La Nuova Italia, 1984). For other aspects of the educational system, see Tina Tomasi, *L'idealismo e fascismo nella scuola italiana* (Florence: La Nuova Italia, 1969); on Gentile, see G. Giraldi, *Giovanni Gentile* (Rome: Armando, 1968); on the Bottai era, Teresa Mezzatosta, *Il regime fascista tra educazione e propaganda, 1935–1943* (Bologna: Cappelli, 1978).

Biographies

There is a growing literature on various Fascist leaders: Claudio Segrè, *Italo Balbo: A Fascist Life* (Berkeley: University of California Press, 1987); the already cited two volume biography of Grandi by Nello, *Dino Grandi: La formazione di un leader fascista* and *Un fedele disubbidiente*, and of Sarfatti by Cannistraro and Sullivan, *Mussolini's Other Woman*; several works by Giordano Bruno Guerri, *Giuseppe Bottai: Un fascista critico* (Milan: Feltrinelli, 1976), *Galeazzo Ciano* (Milan: Bompiani, 1978), and his edited volume, Giuseppe Bottai, *Diario, 1935–1944* (Milan: Rizzoli, 1982). On Farinacci, see Harry Fornari, *Mussolini's Gadfly* (Nashville: Vanderbilt University Press, 1971), and U. Alfassio Grimaldi and Gherardo Bozzetti, *Farinacci, il più fascista* (Milan: Bompiani, 1972); on Renato Ricci, see Sandro Setta, *Renato Ricci: Dallo squadrismo alla Repubblica Sociale Italiana* (Bologna: Il Mulino, 1986); on Gentile, Gabriele Turi, *Giovanni Gentile* (Florence: Giunti, 1995); on Alfredo Rocco, Paolo Ungari, *Alfredo Rocco e l'ideologia giuridica del fascismo* (Brescia: Morcelliana, 1963); and on Victor Emmanuel, Silvio Bertoldi, *Vittorio Emanuele III* (Turin: UTET, 1971). See also Luigi Federzoni's memoir *L'Italia di ieri per la storia di domani* (Milan: Mondadori, 1967); and brief biographies of Balbo, Michele Bianchi, Achille Starace, Augusto Turati, Bottai, Ciano, Federzoni, Rocco, Rossoni, Arrigo Serpieri, and Giuseppe Volpi in *Uomini e volti del fascismo* (Rome: Bulzoni, 1980).

Finally, anyone seeking information on the antifascist Resistance should start with the classic work by Charles Delzell, *Mussolini's Enemies* (Princeton: Princeton University Press, 1961).

Index

CPSIA information can be obtained
at www.ICGtesting.com
Printed in the USA
LVOW13s2226161217
559969LV00022B/628/P